DEAD
PANTIES

DEAD PANTIES

Celia Laratte

iUniverse, Inc.
Bloomington

DEAD PANTIES

iUniverse books may be ordered through booksellers or by contacting:

iUniverse
1663 Liberty Drive
Bloomington, IN 47403
www.iuniverse.com
1-800-Authors (1-800-288-4677)

ISBN: 978-1-4759-5605-4 (sc)
ISBN: 978-1-4759-5606-1 (ebk)

Printed in the United States of America

iUniverse rev. date: 10/10/2012

CONTENTS

I dedicate this book

to my children,
Evans J., Randy E., and Taisha B.;

to my parents,
Manoel R. and Davina;

to my sisters,
Maria L., Maria C., Edna M. (in memoriam),
Maria F., Maria G., Sonia M.;

to my brothers,
Edson (in memoriam), Antonio C., and Jose A.;

and to my nieces,
Priscila and Melina.

And to all those who have helped me
make this dream come true.

ABOUT THE BOOK

The name of this book, *Dead Panties*, was chosen because of what happened to the author's neighbor.

The ex-husband of this woman, whenever he argued with her, would take her panties, cut them up, and then throw them in the trash.

Dead Panties is also an allusion to the death of the sexual appetite of thousands of women who are violated and murdered by their husbands and lovers.

The author says she wrote the book as a way of getting this off her chest and as guidance for young people of both sexes about the dangers of domestic violence, and principally as a way of struggling against the silent violence that permeates homes throughout the world.

May this story influence other people to face the fear and embarrassment and tell people what they are suffering or have suffered from their abusers.

INTRODUCTION

Over the course of history, domestic violence has become a routine occurrence in different parts of the world. Nowadays, this kind of violence has grown like an incurable disease, and all family members suffer, especially the children. Some people ask what domestic violence is, and who better to explain than the victims themselves? I suffered a lot from domestic violence, and my family ended up suffering with me. I had the misfortune of marrying the wrong men, and I went through the worst times of my life with them. That's something I wouldn't wish on anyone, especially a child.

If you'll allow me, I'd like to open the doors to my heart and let you see the many scars it bears. I often wonder if someday there will be a cure, but I know that this cure has to begin with me.

But there are also good things in my life, like my family, who I would like to introduce to you.

My name is Celia Laratte. I was born in Salvador Bahia, Brazil, and I am proud to be Brazilian. But for over twenty years I have lived in the United States of America. I come from a humble family of six sisters and three brothers, with great parents who were with us until the last days of their lives. Dad was a great mechanic, working for Petrobras, one of the biggest companies in Brazil, and my mother was an excellent seamstress, cook, and confectioner. Together, these two magnificent people gave us the best of everything.

We went through the good and the bad for many years, but my parents dedicated their lives to all of us. Dad worked two jobs to feed the ten children. Sometimes we had breakfast but no lunch or dinner, but we were united and very happy, especially when we were all together at home. Despite the difficulties, our parents raised us to be good men and women.

I distinctly remember how my sister Lourdes, the eldest, helped us both educationally and financially. We were all grateful for this, and she is now happily married to her partner, a marvelous person, in a big house they built themselves.

My late brother Edson was the second child, and Dad did all he could to make him a good man. He was extremely smart, even speaking English and French in high school, but he never finished his education due to other priorities in his life. He had to start working to support his own family. When his first daughter, my niece Ana Cristina (now a brilliant teacher), was born, it was an extremely happy event for all of us, especially my parents and sisters. My parents helped care for their granddaughter, and she ended up living with her grandparents. Edson had four children, who now pursue their own careers and have their own families.

My sister Carmem was a manicurist by profession, an exquisite worker, who married a man very dear to our parents in a beautiful ceremony. A while back, he became very sick, but, thankfully, his health has now improved. They have children and now have several grandchildren.

My fourth sister, Edna, passed away; she was always the most distant from the family. She married, had five children, and lived happily with her family.

Antonio Carlos, my brother, is a very intelligent man; he has traveled all over the world and served in the army for several years. He has ten children, all of whom are studying and living their lives well.

Maria das Graças (Gracinha) is one of my closest sisters. We have always been very close, ever since we were young, and as a result, when I left my parents, I promised that one day she would come and live with me in the United States. Some years later, this promise was fulfilled. Gracinha is very intelligent and hardworking and is doing very well here. When she arrived, seventeen years ago, she didn't want to stay at all and thought of nothing but returning home. Eventually, she met her Prince Charming and fell in love. After a while, they moved in together and had a child, and my niece Taisha was born, making them both very happy.

Jose Augusto, another brother, was a quiet, shy boy who never left the house because he was embarrassed to wear new clothes. Now he is married, very elegant, and a great mechanic. Retired with four children, he lives happily with his family.

Fatima, another sister, is a foodie. I have never known such a calm person my entire life, and she is like that with everyone. When it comes to the kitchen, she is a master, and her business is expanding rapidly. She trained as a high school teacher, is married, and is a great mother to her two marvelous daughters. Suanei, the elder, is very intelligent, went to college, and works at one of the best companies in our country. Priscila is, in my opinion, the most beautiful girl in the world, and, in fact, she was selected Ile Aiye Carnival Queen in 2001. She was chosen from an array of competing girls to represent the most traditional Bahian carnival group in Latin America in terms of African culture. I thank God for them; they deserve the best.

Sonia is the baby of the family and a genius. I never thought such a smart person could exist. She loves to study, graduated from college, and completed courses in English and tourism. She continues studying to be a history teacher. She works for the largest oil company in the country and is very dedicated to her work. Although she is so busy, she always finds time to train every morning, as she competes in races both in Bahia and further afield. She is very courageous and has finished first or second in many events. Aside from all these activities, she also has a husband and a daughter named Melina.

Chapter 1

CELESTINA'S STORY

Celestina was the fifth daughter of the family and always had an air of superiority; she was kind of a macho, daredevil woman. She was always close to her father. Wherever he went, he took her with him, because he knew she'd help him with anything he needed. She adored her father, he was the hero of the family, and she thought he was the best dad in the world. He was a man of strong and elegant character. He was a brave, respectful man, who, in turn, was respected by everyone. Celestina learned a lot from him and always wanted a piece of his intelligence. Thanks to him, she managed to get it; she was always good at math in school.

Celestina loved to write poems. As she didn't have any money to buy presents, whenever it was someone's birthday in the family, she wrote a poem as a gift. Whenever she read one at a birthday party, she often started crying, and many of those attending cried too. She became known in the neighborhood and was invited to write poems for all kinds of celebrations. Because of this, she became known as a teacher. She also had the chance to sing in the school choir, which led to her being on television. She was a hardworking girl but didn't get very far, perhaps due to the lack of incentive from the adults in her life. She finished primary school and high school and took two years of accounting classes before she left college.

Back then, life wasn't like it is now. The only job Celestina could get was in a factory sewing blue jeans. She worked for a few years in the factory, and then she took a job in a drugstore. While working there, she had more freedom to go out alone, and soon she met Roberto, the cousin of a friend of hers. Celestina fell in love for the first time in her life. He was always at her parents' house, and she was always at his, but nothing ever happened between them. One day, they went to the beach and he asked if he could touch her breasts; she refused, perhaps due to her innocence. But from that day on, she lost any good feelings that she had for him; deep down, she thought he only wanted to take advantage of her.

And then Celestina met Jose, a friend of her brother's who worked at a cafeteria. She didn't like him very much, but he was so persistent that she agreed to date him. Celestina's dad didn't approve of him, because Jose was not educated. When her parents expressed the opinion that he wasn't good enough for her, she started to like him. Perhaps if her parents had approved, she wouldn't have stayed with him. They became engaged, and after four years, they decided to get married, but it turned into a disaster. She had to arrange everything: she paid the rent for the house they lived in, and she had to ask her aunt Celina to buy them furniture on credit and pay for the food and drink for the wedding, her bridal dress, his tux, and the rings. All this was without any help from her parents, who didn't want her to get married. When her wedding day arrived, she was married without them there.

After the wedding, she and Jose went home. It wasn't really a home, it seemed more like a matchbox, but at the time there was nothing more important than how they felt. They had some loving moments during their first nights. After a few months, differences began to appear. Jose was not working; never having a fixed job, he preferred to work off and on as a street vendor. The electricity was shut off, but thank goodness, she continued working to pay the bills. It didn't bother Celestina that she didn't feel loved, and they lived like that for a long time. One day, when they were out for a walk, they met her sister-in-law, who was married to her brother; she invited them to her birthday party. Celestina was happy because she hadn't had any fun in a long time, and she knew that almost everyone in her family would be there. She was really looking forward to it. On the day of the party, they got ready and left early because they had to walk there; as she imagined, everyone was there having a great time.

They talked and danced, had some drinks, and soon time passed. She was dancing with her cousin when Jose, who was already drunk, got jealous and began to push her. She fell to the floor, but that was not enough for him; he picked her up, slapped her across the face, and began to tear her clothes. When her brother saw what was happening, he became enraged and threw Jose out. The house was transformed into hell; they had to call an ambulance for her because there was an enormous cut on her lip, but she didn't need any stitches and they let her go.

When she got home, Jose was waiting for her. He shoved her roughly onto the bed and began to rape her. She lay still, as stiff as a board, without moving an inch, as tears rolled down her cheeks. At that moment, she wanted to die. When he was satisfied, he pushed her away and fell asleep. Celestina got up to wash her private parts and sat on a chair, waiting for morning to come. When she saw the light of dawn approaching, she walked out the door and went to her parents' house. She spent the whole day there, introverted, wanting and not wanting to go back; for some reason she missed Jose and thought it was strange he hadn't come get her. By nightfall, there was a knock at the door, and it was him. It only took some apologies and a few kisses, and she decided to return home. When they got home, they made love, and everything returned to normal. Things were good for a long time, because he swore that never again in his life would he touch her that way.

How she wanted it to be true. The saying goes that those who commit abuse once will never stop doing it, and that is indeed what happened; he abused her again. This time, because she was tired and refused to have sex, he sent her straight to hospital with a blow to the head. She had fifteen stitches and lost so much blood that she had to have a transfusion and stay in hospital for almost a week. He went to visit her a few times but wasn't allowed in. When she was released, she went to her parents' house to recover. As it was serious, they had a big meeting with the entire family, and they told her that if she didn't want to go back and live with Jose, she could live with them forever. And that is what she decided to do.

The days went by and she was getting better each day, until she was finally well enough to go back to work. Celestina felt like a new person. One day after work, Jose came over and began begging her to come back, saying he was no longer the same violent man and asking her to please forgive him. She realized that she could no longer stand him and didn't want to be abused by him or any other man. She then suggested to her parents that it would be best for her to go to another part of the country, and they agreed with her.

She arranged everything and left for Rio de Janeiro, where she stayed with Omar, a friend of her aunt Celina. Omar was a lady who dressed like a *baiana* (traditionally dressed woman from the state of Bahia) and sold *acaraje* (traditional dish, originally from Africa, using deep-fried bean mix) in the square. It was just the two of them, and while Omar worked, Celestina was alone, but they helped one other. After a while, Omar introduced her to her nephew Pedro, who was almost the same age as Celestina. He took her out to show her the city, and they began to to the movies, to the theater, and to parties. They kissed sometimes, but nothing serious. Pedro wanted more than a friendship, but she wasn't ready yet, so he left.

Celestina told Omar that she wanted a job, to get some money and buy things that she needed; her dad sent her some money every now and then, but it wasn't much, since he couldn't afford any more.

She looked for work every day. Day after day, she returned home with aching feet. One day, when she got home, she found a letter from Jose, which made her blood run cold. Celestina couldn't understand how he had gotten her address. She called her relatives and asked if they knew how Jose had got hold of her address, and they didn't know either, but they warned her never to answer his letters. And that is what she did.

He wrote that he missed her, that he wanted her to come back, and that he no longer lived at home because her dad had returned all the furniture to the store, since he couldn't pay for it. He also wrote that he was unemployed, and she knew that in his next letter he would ask to come and live with her. He said it was time for them to restart their lives. When she read this, she felt afraid and panicked, and the only thing she thought about was leaving the country forever.

Her Aunt Celina was already living in the United States of America; she had been working as a maid for a Brazilian politician, and when he was transferred to the Brazilian embassy in the United States, he asked her to go with him and his family. He explained that he would be at the US embassy for four years, and she replied that she didn't know if she could be so far from her sister and nephews for so long, as she was godmother to seven of her sister's ten children. Eventually, she decided to go with him, since it was a dream of her to go to America.

So Celestina wrote her aunt a letter, explaining everything that had happened to her and asking if she could join her. Initially, Celina's answer was no, because Celestina was very young and she wouldn't be able to live with her, as she only had a room in the embassy. Eventually she agreed to the idea, saying she would try to get her a job as a maid, and Celestina was very happy. Celina asked around and found a diplomat who needed a maid.

Celestina thought she would be able to travel a few days later, but she needed to get a passport and visa in order to leave Brazil, and it took a year for the papers to be completed. Every week she had to get up at four in the morning and stand in an enormous line, hoping that her documents would be ready. Then one day they told her that her passport and visa was ready. She cried so much with joy, thanked everyone, and went back to Omar's house to prepare for her trip.

In February 1976, with pain in her heart and great sadness, because no one from her family could say good-bye to her at the airport, Celestina left Brazil to forget her past and find a new life in the United States.

Chapter 2

IN THE UNITED STATES OF AMERICA

Celestina was shaking like a leaf on the plane, as it was the first time in her entire life she had flown. She put her things away and nervously began to pray, not just for herself but for all those there on the plane. During the trip, her thoughts wandered to her new life and imagined what it would be like in the United States. Would she be able to get used to living in a new country? How much would she miss her family? At the same time, she thought this trip would be good for everyone.

When the plane landed in New York, she felt a little bit sad. At the airport, she was met by Irene, a friend of her aunt Celina. They hugged and she asked her about everyone in Brazil, and then she took Celestina to her apartment, where she tidied herself up. After resting, she took her to see a bit of the city. Celestina was struck by the cold weather, and after a good walk, they returned and went to sleep, as the next day she was going to Washington to meet up with her aunt Celina.

The next day, Irene took Celestina to the bus station, and a few hours later, she was in the capital of the United States, meeting her aunt, who she hadn't seen for many years. Celina couldn't believe she was finally reunited with one of her favorite nieces. When they had finished hugging and kissing, they took a taxi to the Brazilian embassy, where Celina lived. They met her friends, who were waiting for them with a good *feijoada* (the Brazilian national dish, of beans and different kinds of meat), and they spent a long time talking about everything and catching up.

The next morning, Celestina began her new life as a maid. Mrs. Matilde, her new boss, drove Celestina to her house, where she met her mother, Julia; her two daughters, Monica and Margarita; and her husband. They seemed like a normal family, and Celestina thought everything would work out fine.

But things did not go as she expected. Mrs. Matilde acted as if she ruled the world; she was the kind of person born into misery who, when they succeed in life, likes to step on others. She didn't allow Celestina near the children, and any dishes Celestina washed, she washed again in the dishwasher. She told Celestina that black people were born to be slaves, and ordered her to eat behind the house (she could never sit anywhere in the house to eat). Celestina cried a lot; she had read about slaves in history books at high school, but she didn't know slavery existed in real life today. From that moment on, her life became hell; sometimes she wasn't given food, she couldn't take a bath in the house, and she often slept in the yard, with no blanket; when morning broke, she would wake her up with a bucket of cold water in her face.

Mrs. Matilde made it quite clear that not even in her wildest dreams was she to touch the telephone to make a call. One day, everyone was out and she was alone in the house. Celestina couldn't stand being mistreated anymore, so she went up to Mrs. Matilde's room, as that was the only room with a telephone, and called Pedro, a friend in Brazil, to tell him what was happening to her here.

Pedro didn't say much, because he was also shocked that slavery still existed. As she talked, she heard someone coming. Celestina ran downstairs, and there was Mrs. Matilde, who knew from her face that she'd done something wrong. She went up to her room and when she came down, she slapped her across the face demanded that Celestina tell her what she was doing in her room. With no other alternative, Celestina told her the truth; that she had used the telephone to call her friend in Brazil.

The woman turned into a demon, hitting her so hard she lost a tooth. She called Celestina's aunt, saying she could only stay in her house until the telephone bill arrived, as she needed to know how much the phone call had cost, and she should thank God Mrs. Matilde hadn't called the police.

Aunt Celina was so upset she became ill. When the telephone bill arrived, it was very expensive and Mrs. Matilde kept all Celestina's wages, and then she threw her out of her house like a street dog.

She left crying like a madwoman, knowing she'd done wrong in making the call, but thinking the punishment did not fit the crime. She also was worried that Aunt Celina would make her go back to Brazil. She was very afraid, because she wanted to continue being able to help the family she had left there. Thankfully, she let her stay, and a few days later, she was able to find another Brazilian family to work for.

Her new boss's name was Sandra, who lived with her husband, Ronaldo, and her two children, Marcos and Marcelo. This job was a bit better, because everyone went out to work and she stayed at home with Marcelo, while Marcos went to school. She was able to do everything there, but she felt good because they treated her well, and she wondered how two Brazilian women could be so utterly different.

In time, she forgot about all the bad times she had with Mrs. Matilde, but traces of her ill deeds remained. Aunt Celina continued to feel ill and went to the doctor, but they couldn't find anything wrong. However, one day, someone at the embassy called Sandra's house to say that Celina had died. Forlorn, Celestina couldn't believe that she had only been in the United States six months, and her aunt was no longer there with her. She thought about what she would do here, without knowing anybody, but she stayed. After Celina's body was sent back to Brazil, Celestina moved to New York. She left Washington with only twenty dollars in her purse. She had made plans to meet Vilma, a friend of her mother, at the station, but when she got to New York, she couldn't find her. Celestina stayed in the bus station for more than a week, and she began to look like a beggar, since she couldn't take a bath; she couldn't even call her family in Brazil.

One day, she was sitting on the station platform, crying like a child, when a lady came up and, speaking in English, asked what was wrong. Celestina explained in Portuguese that she spoke no English, but then a miracle happened, because the lady was also Brazilian and spoke Portuguese. Celestina began to tell the woman, named Wanda, everything that had happened to her, and then she took Celestina to her house, where she had a bath, changed clothes, ate, and slept the whole day, because she was so tired and troubled. The next day, they had breakfast and went out to look for Vilma. They walked around until they finally found her. Celestina thanked Wanda, and they said good-bye.

Celestina went back to Vilma's apartment; she and her friend Joice had been very worried about her, not knowing how to find her, but everything turned out all right. Celestina lived with them for a few months; Vilma found her a job cleaning houses, which was just enough to get by, but in a few weeks, she managed to save enough money to pay an agency to find her a job in an old people's home.

This place was like a home away from home. Some of these people had had their own families, but as they grew older, their children didn't want the responsibility of taking care of them and had left them there. It wasn't really a bad place. They were happy and had a lot of fun activities. Her job was to clean thirty-one rooms, seven days a week, with room and board. She arrived there a few days before Christmas in 1977, without knowing anybody. Celestina was happy, because at least she was working, but she could stay in her room and do whatever she wanted. She was also sad because she was alone, especially on Christmas Day. Celestina saw snow falling for the first time; it was the most beautiful thing in the world and encouraged her to go on working. She became a completely different person. She started to mature and think like an adult.

When she met some of the other employees, she was surprised to find people from many different countries. There were Puerto Ricans, Dominicans, and Brazilians. What a joy! It was then she began to believe that God would always be by her side.

How good it was to meet people who spoke the same language, because Celestina really didn't know any English. When they finished work, they met up again to get to know each other better.

One of her coworkers, Antonia, had been in the United States for many years; she lived in Manhattan with her aunt, her children, and her nieces. They all lived together, and at the end of the week, Celestina went to Manhattan with her to share the warmth of their home. Antonia defended Celestina from everything and everyone; they were always together and were inseparable. She went to her niece's wedding, to her son's baptism, and to other family events. They spent the holidays together, but one Christmas night, when they got to her house, something terrible had happened. Her niece had climbed to the sixth floor of the building and jumped off; the poor thing had died instantly.

Oh God, how sad. Celestina had never seen anything like it up close; she thought such things only happened on television news and in the newspapers. The niece was just fifteen, a beautiful healthy girl, and they never found out why she did this terrible thing. As a result of this tragic accident, Antonia had to leave her job, as the pain was too great.

Celestina continued working and was even promoted, as another colleague left her job. She became a supervisor, taking all the towels and checking the rooms.

Her coworkers were from Spain, Colombia, Mexico, Ecuador, Cuba, or some other country; they were good and bad people, which really taught her about life. She saw everything; drugs were everywhere, and she was offered them time and again, but she was strong enough not to fall into temptation. It would have been easy for her to fall into the abyss, as she was alone, leading her own life, with no one to tell her what to do, but she didn't. Celestina had everything planned in her head. She had a mission to fulfill for herself and her family, and that's how it would be. She had come to work, and nothing could make her forget it. She never fell into temptation. One afternoon at work, as she was looking out the window, something unexpected happened.

From the window, she saw a Camaro pull up, and a young man got out and came into the hotel. Celestina ran downstairs to see who he was, and she saw him talking to Mrs. Lane, the hotel owner. She walked past them, as if nothing was happening, and went to the soda machine, bought a soda, walked back upstairs. He said good-bye to Mrs. Lane and came after her. He asked if she worked there and for how long, and she asked why he wanted to know. He said he was thinking of coming to work at the hotel. Then he asked her name and where she was from. She replied her name was Celestina and she was Brazilian, and all of a sudden, he took her hand and asked, "Will you marry me?"

"How can I marry you?" she replied. "We've only known each other a few minutes. I don't even know your name."

So he introduced himself; his name was Rafael. After they chatted a while, he said good-bye and left. She wondered if she would see him again or if it was just a dream.

The next day at work, Celestina thought about him all day, waiting anxiously for the afternoon to come and to see if he would come by; she was dying to see him again. That afternoon, as she sat at the window, there he was again. She went down to see him again, and she asked him who he had come to see at the hotel. He said his friend Edivaldo worked there, and they had worked together before. After they talked for a few minutes, he said good-bye and left.

For the next few days, they followed the same routine. After about a month, he invited her on a date, and she happily accepted. The night before their date, she couldn't sleep at all, and when he came to pick her up, she was shaking like a leaf and so nervous she couldn't speak. The only thing she could say was hello, and they began getting to know each other. After a few hours, he brought her back home and said good-bye. From that day on, they began to go out more frequently. One day they decided to go to the park, where they kissed and touched for hours and hours. She started to get hot and feel the butterflies we all feel when we start to fall in love; she asked him to take her someplace private. They went to a motel, and when they went into the room, she caught Rafael squeezing the pillows to find the softest one for himself.

She thought it was pretty selfish of him, but she didn't take it very seriously. They continued dating, and after a few months, he started to sleep in her room every weekend, arriving on Friday afternoons and only leaving on Monday mornings.

Everything was going well until Celestina went to look for Rafael in the hotel where he worked. When she rang the doorbell, he came to the door without a shirt and with the zipper of his pants undone. Worst of all, he wouldn't let her into his room, because he was with Vanda, his other girlfriend. She didn't make a fuss or say anything to him, she called a taxi and returned to her room. Later, he turned up with a thousand excuses; Celestina forgave him and eventually forgot what had happened.

Her love for him grew day by day without her realizing it, so much so that sometimes she couldn't sleep if he wasn't in the room with her. Celestina often stayed awake all night, wondering where he was and with whom. One day, she learned that he had another girlfriend, and her family wanted them to marry, but he hadn't agreed to it. They had known each other many years, but he told Celestina that he didn't really love her. Celestina was somewhat relieved, and they carried on with their lives.

Things started getting serious between them. He taught her to drive, he helped her get her driver's license, and then they decided to buy a used car together. The car cost them $3,000, and she gave him half, thinking the car would be hers. To Celestina's surprise, he gave her his old car and kept the one they had bought. At the time, she thought nothing but good of him; she still thought he was the ideal person for her, until one fine day, as she was driving to an appointment, she saw someone else driving their car. She followed the car to a car wash. She waited outside, and to her surprise, she saw that the driver was Vanda.

Despondent, Celestina forgot about her appointment and returned to her room. She was disappointed, because Rafael never let her, who'd helped pay for the car, touch the keys, let alone drive it. It hurt her so much that she told him that she had had enough and it was all over. He swore to her that he had nothing to do with Vanda, that she had only offered to take the car to be washed because he was very busy with work.

Celestina didn't believe him anymore, but as she didn't want to lose him, she said nothing.

Around this time, she felt the need to have someone from her family close, and she invited her sister Marta to come and live with her. She was Celestina's best friend, and she had promised to bring her to the United States. She needed someone to talk to, due to the fact that she was feeling very alone. In just a few months, Marta came to America and moved in with Celestina. Mrs. Lane agreed to hire Marta, and they worked together for a few years. One day, however, a new supervisor was hired, and she managed to convince Mrs. Lane to fire Celestina and her sister; after she had worked there for seven years, she was told that their services were no longer required, and they needed to find another place to live.

Celestina didn't know what to do, as this had been a big surprise. Celestina and Marta looked for an apartment, and soon they found one to share with Rafael, who was the only one with a job. Marta and Celestina they found a job close to their new apartment. It was in a factory making bathroom deodorant, a blue and green liquid. It was a hell of a job because they could taste it in their food, and they spat blue or green, depending on the color they were working on that day. Everywhere they went, they left paint marks, and worst of all, they couldn't do anything because it was the only job they could find, and they needed it to pay their bills.

With their first paycheck, they sat down to decide how they would pay their bills and they reached an agreement.

Rafael agreed to put the electricity and house in his name, with each of them giving him their share of the expenses. One day, however, Rafael lost his job, and he spent the next few months looking for another. So as not to be idle, he worked at a building site fairly far from home. It took him hours to drive there and back, and it wasn't worth it, as he fell off a ladder and broke his foot. Celestina didn't know that a man could be so weak; he didn't leave her in peace for a single minute. He was like a one-year-old child, calling her for everything, and she just about went crazy.

After almost a year, things began to return to normal. Rafael managed to get a job in an institution, taking care of people with mental illness, and he was very happy. This was the moment she had been waiting for: she was ready to have a child, but that was something he had never wanted. They tried, but she was unable to become pregnant, and they didn't know why. She went to Dr. Barry, her gynecologist, who did some tests but found nothing unusual. The doctor suggested they go to a clinic to find out if the problem lay with Rafael. However, those tests were negative, which meant everything was fine with him, and the problem probably lay with her.

When she went back to Dr. Barry, she was worried that she couldn't have children, but he gave her hope, saying that perhaps there was a problem that could be solved, and he set an appointment to run some more tests.

She went to the hospital for these tests. When the results arrived, Dr. Barry told her there was a small problem, but she shouldn't worry, as it wasn't too serious. Celestina's uterus was blocked by a tumor, but it was benign. She needed a small operation, but he guaranteed that in a few months, she could become pregnant. She agreed to the surgery and they immediately took her to the operating room, where they removed the tumor. She stayed in hospital for observation and after four days, they let her out.

At home, she followed Dr. Barry's instructions, and in a week she was well again. Months and months passed, and then a year, and nothing, but she never lost hope, and after two years, she became pregnant. It was the happiest day of her life; she called everyone in her family and told all her friends the news, but there was one person who wasn't too enthusiastic. Rafael never wanted the responsibility of raising a child. She didn't think too much of it, because she planned to have this child with or without his support. During her nine months of pregnancy, Rafael's involvement was minimal. Once in a while, he would take her to a restaurant for those late night food desires, but mostly she relied on Marta; without her she would have been helpless. He always was a disinterested and cold man.

All her wishes came true. On November 25, 1982, her son was born. He was a healthy and complete boy. At his father's request, they named him Elvis. Being a mother was the most marvelous experience in the world for Celestina, especially when she felt her baby move inside of her. It was a sensation she would forget and another reason to love him with every bone in her body. She would fight tooth and nail to make sure that he never went without.

Marta and Celestina took turns looking after the baby. Marta took great care of him when Celestina went out to work. Elvis was a very lucky, well-protected child, and he never needed to go to hospital for anything; he never fell, he never had a cold, and his health was always very good. These were some of the best years of their lives, and soon, Celestina wanted another child. Two years later, Celestina became pregnant again, but she had to make a tough decision. She had just been hired for a better job, and Rafael encouraged her to have an abortion, saying it wouldn't be a good idea to start working when she was pregnant. Celestina didn't know how she fell for his line, but she did. At that time she didn't have much life experience, and she believed him when he said they wouldn't employ a pregnant woman.

All lies! When she started working, she met a pregnant colleague and asked her how she managed to get work. Her response left Celestina dumbstruck. She said Celestina shouldn't be fooled by anyone, this was the United States of America and a pregnant woman could get a job anywhere. She was very sad at having terminated her pregnancy and asked God to forgive her ignorance. From that moment on, she decided to become a different person and make her own decisions. She learned many things in this job, and in 1985 she became pregnant again and decided to keep this child.

Every month she went for a prenatal appointment, but she was very stressed out. At six months she went to see Dr. Barry as usual, and when he took her blood pressure, it was so high he sent her to the hospital there and then. He was afraid that something would happen to the child. When Celestina arrived at the hospital, she was admitted immediately, as her blood pressure was through the roof and would not go down. After a week in the hospital, the child stopped moving in her belly, and when they took her for an ultrasound, they found that the child had died. It felt like punishment from God for the abortion she had. The birth was induced, and they took him away to be buried.

The next day she returned home alone. She cried for days and locked herself in her room; she couldn't bear people's questions about what was going on. But as she couldn't hide away forever, she decided to return to work, and her colleagues treated her with great kindness and understanding. A few months later, Celestina was feeling much better, but she could never forget those two events that happened to her. She knew that she would have to let go and perhaps try again in the future; God might take pity on her.

And so it was in 1986 that she became pregnant once again. As always, she went to see a doctor, but not Dr. Barry, as she no longer trusted him. She knew that it wasn't his fault, but she thought he could have done more to save her baby. The first doctor she met refused to see her, saying he didn't have the means to deliver the baby to someone considered high risk, due to her age and high blood pressure; he recommended another hospital that cared for pregnant women with this kind of problem.

At Westchester Hospital she met Dr. Camilo, who told her that she needed to take blood pressure medication throughout the nine months of the pregnancy and be examined every week until the birth. After six months, Dr. Camilo examined the amniotic fluid, as he feared that, due to the medication she was on, the child would be born with a physical defect. But one week later, the results came back normal; she was expecting another boy. When she found out the child was in good health, she was happy, but she was also sad, because she wanted a girl. She lost the will to be a mother and asked the doctor to take this child out of her as quickly as possible. Dr. Camilo replied that he couldn't do that; she would have to wait the nine months for him to be born.

On August 26, 1987, she was admitted to hospital for a normal birth the next day. Things got complicated as her blood pressure rose a lot, and the anesthetic wasn't working. Dr. Camilo wanted her to be awake, but things were becoming so dangerous that he decided to put her out, and at ten o'clock the next morning, August 27, Roger was born, a healthy boy weighing around seven and a half pounds. But Celestina wasn't well; she lost a lot of blood and needed a transfusion. She was in critical condition, and the doctor didn't know if she would survive. The case was so serious that Dr. Camilo himself stayed there the whole night until daybreak, to be absolutely sure that all the danger had passed. He saved her life, but she returned home knowing that she could never have another child. She had to have her tubes sealed, but although she was sad, her health had to come first.

Their second-floor apartment was already rather cozy, housing her sister Marta and her boyfriend Dave in one room, and Celestina, Rafael, Elvis, and Roger in the other. It was a squeeze for all of them, and as Rafael didn't move, Celestina decided to get another job. A friend introduced her to one of his supervisors; the same day, she filled out an application. When she handed it in the next day, the supervisor asked her how soon she could start; Celestina replied, "Right now, if you like."

Celestina started working at the Mental Disability Corporation; because of this job, they were able to look for a house to buy. Their mortgage application was approved, which hadn't happened before as their income wasn't sufficient. With this second job, her spirits rose, and they found a bigger house, with more space. It had three bedrooms, one bathroom, a living room, kitchen, and a small yard. She was very happy and proud because she knew that due to her will to move forward, her children would have more space to play. She felt a big difference when she moved to this house.

Chapter 3

NEW HOME, NEW LIFE

It was in the new house that Celestina really began to get to know what kind of person Rafael really was. Marta had decided to rent a studio flat in the same building for her and her boyfriend. It was better that way, because they needed to start living their own lives. Soon after moving in, Rafael introduced lots of rules: lights out in all parts of the house, day and night, only to be used when essential; when taking a bath, turn off the taps when soaping; when brushing teeth, use a small cup of water; don't leave the taps on in the bath; urinate several times before flushing. Celestina wondered what kind of life other people would be leading if they had two small children. She was sorry, but that wasn't the way it was going to be. She was working two jobs, not him; her children hadn't asked to be born, and she would never let them suffer for material things.

Rafael was a cold man, vulgar and cynical, with a very primitive way of thinking. He was a liar, who drew conclusions from things without knowing what was going on. Gradually, she realized what he was like; if it were today, she swore she wouldn't hesitate to say no to him. Celestina didn't know what planet he came from or what kind of family brought him up, because when she thought about her family, there was no comparison. They were a very close family, and she promised herself that her children would follow in her footsteps; no one could do otherwise.

Elvis was a reserved child, perhaps because of his father's ill treatment. Throughout his childhood he had problems at school, the teachers called Celestina constantly, as he was very quiet in the classroom and had greater difficulty learning than the other pupils. He was put in a class with other children with learning difficulties. More often than not, parents don't think about how they speak and act toward their children may harm them. Rafael acted as though Elvis was his servant, making him take a bath at two o'clock in the morning to sharpen his memory, or waking him at six o'clock in the morning to study, saying it was the best time to learn. He always liked to compare him to others, saying that this one or that one was better than him, even making plans for Roger's future, because he was more intelligent than Elvis.

Celestina's children had a very sad childhood. They grew up without fatherly love, without a father they could communicate with, or ask for help, or even ask for advice. Mainly, they grew up without a father who was a friend. Rafael only cared about what he wanted to do and expected Celestina to agree with every stupid thing he did with the children. She always told him that if he wanted her to remain his wife forever, he should stop mistreating her children, they didn't ask to be born.

She was courageous despite her fear. She always defended her children, always tried to listen to them, and always showed them love and affection. Deep down, she considered herself the happiest mother in the world, for having their trust and friendship. She didn't think of them as her children, but her best friends; she was blessed that they asked her for advice, her opinion, her help. They often sat together telling jokes and laughing heartily, and they understood each other, but then they would hear the door open. Rafael would come in, and they took different paths. For example, if they were in the living room talking, she would lay down on the couch and pretend to be asleep; Roger would run upstairs and go on the computer; and Elvis would lock himself in his room and open the door for no one. It's very sad that someone can do so much harm to their own family.

In 1996, after many years without seeing her family, she received a call from Laura, her eldest sister in Brazil, saying she and Carla, another sister, were coming to visit. They had received their share of the inheritance from their father, who had died a few years earlier. When Celestina received this news, she was very happy, but deep down she worried about how Rafael would behave around her sisters. Celestina talked to him and begged him to treat them well, as she had treated his mother and sister, who lived with them for a few months. He promised that he would treat them well, especially Carla, who had had a stroke a few years back and could not even talk properly.

A week later. Rafael drove Celestina, Marta, her niece, Roger, and Elvis to the airport to pick them up. It was very emotional, seeing them again after so many years. They remembered lots of things from the past, sharing laughter and tears, but they were very happy. On her free time, she took them sightseeing in New York, which left them thrilled and happy. But one day, Laura complained to Marta that the previous night, as she and Carla were sleeping, Rafael woke up Roger and Elvis and ordered them to come in and switch off the air conditioner.

Marta grew angry and asked Rafael, "How can you be so mean? For the love of God, don't do that, have a bit of compassion, it's really hot."

She was working that night and the telephone rang; she heard a lot of shouting and asked what was going on. She already imagined that Rafael was the cause of the problem. He ordered Elvis to explain to her on the phone, but before this, the wretch had made the children think he was acting correctly, because he didn't want their visitors to catch cold. How kind of him!

It was then she found out about things that were going on in her absence. He made their lives impossible, watching over everything they did, including when and how much they ate. Terrified, because in her mind he had overstepped the mark, she felt awful and, thoroughly embarrassed, sat down with them and asked for forgiveness a thousand and one times. She told them things they never knew about her and the life she led with this abuser. She also told Laura that he managed all of her money, including signing her checks and making whatever transactions he wanted.

Laura asked Celestina if she was crazy and told her, for the love of God, to leave the idiot because he would leave her with absolutely nothing. And that is exactly what happened. As they already had so many problems and everything had to be as he wanted, she never had the right to choose anything for her house, not even with her own money.

She decided to follow Laura's advice, and after a big argument with Rafael, she asked him to separate their money at the bank. He had no problem doing what she had asked; he went to the bank and returned with $6,000. In her bank account alone, there had been over $20,000 (she had received a settlement due to a car accident she had suffered with him; he had also received over $10,000). She couldn't believe he was doing all this to her, and she fell into a depression, which almost drove her crazy.

It was then that Celestina decided to become independent; she opened her own bank account, in her and the children's name, and started over. How could such mean people exist? Women should not trust their men. There is no love on many of their parts; they are looking out for themselves. When some women love, they surrender themselves from head to toe and are sincere about how they feel. Celestina was like that until she decided to stop, think, and take control of her own life, alone from then on. Deep, deep down, she had always been alone; he only did things because he had access to her money.

From then on, Rafael became a demon, and the problems increased. She had to learn how to do everything, as if she was just starting to read and write, because he'd made her useless, good for nothing, and it was him who had to be on top of everything. Celestina had thought this was normal, but it wasn't, and so she had to ask her sister Marta and her best friend Matheu to help. They taught her how to open a bank account, how to fill out a check, how to get a credit card, how to look after her car insurance, and much, much more.

She had known Matheu for many years; they worked together, and he was good for her. He seemed sincere and respectful; he treated her well and also gave her advice. It was as if God had put him in her path to motivate her toward something, and they learned a lot from each other. Whenever Celestina had a problem with Rafael, she asked his advice, and he always listened to her. Matheu had also been advising her to save a little money in the bank, but Rafael always said her money wasn't even enough to pay the bills. She tried many, many times, unsuccessfully, and so she let it go. Another thing she owed to Matheu: he encouraged her to quit smoking. She almost destroyed her health by smoking; due to the depression she was suffering, she smoked two packs of cigarettes a day, sometimes more.

First of all, she must thank God, then him, for all the advice he gave her, especially when he told Celestina that if she really loved her children, she had to be with them every step of the way and see them grow. This moved her so much that even he couldn't believe it. She quit smoking without any medication, but with great willpower. Celestina will live a few more years because of this and much more, for which she will be grateful to Matheu for the rest of her life. On the other hand, she suffered a lot because Rafael accused her of being Matheu's lover. Celestina could not understand how he believed it all; it was like he had a great weight on his own conscience; in spite of everything, the wretch still threatened her, saying he would call Matheu's wife to say that she was seeing her husband.

At the beginning, when he threatened her with this slander, she was very afraid and embarrassed because she didn't know how his wife would react. They talked to each other, they weren't the best of friends, but they knew each other well. Rafael tarnished her reputation, telling everybody Matheu and she were together, that he had destroyed his family. What a liar! He'd destroyed it himself, because Matheu only gave Celestina advice. She had some bad times, was outcast by everyone, because his rumors had spread like a contagious disease. She didn't think there was a cure for this kind of malice. But God was behind her, lighting her path to continue struggling against everything and everyone.

Celestina tried, but the pressure was too much for her. She couldn't stand the problems she was facing and ended up going to a psychologist. She began losing interest in everything; she didn't care about anything, she just cried. She didn't know where so many tears were coming from, and all the time, she thought she was going crazy. She asked God what was happening and what evil she had done to pay such a high price! She started by thinking of her children, that they needed her and there was no one better to bring them up than herself, so she began praying every day and talking to a psychologist three times a week. Little by little, Celestina improved and, God willing, one day she believed she would be well.

While she was trying to get better, Celestina received a phone call at home. The person on the line hung up when she said hello, and after a few minutes the phone rang again. This time she was slightly aggressive when she answered, and a woman's voice asked for Rafael. It was Vanda. Some years ago, before he and Celestina were married, Vanda was separated from her husband and had given up her life for him. Rafael was also the kind of man who liked to live off women, and she promised him the world, including a new car. He thought that he was good looking and could attract many women. Nowadays, as far as Celestina was concerned, he was ignorant and very ill-bred, without morals or scruples.

His other girlfriend was Sandra, a friend of his sister. Celestina and Rafael were already married with their first son. When Elvis was five years old, Rafael would bring him to her house and put him in the living room to watch television while he went into her bedroom to have sex with her. This went on for a long time. How embarrassing; what kind of example did this guy think he was setting for his child? He was with this woman for a long time, and one day when Celestina was shopping with her sister, she saw Rafael with Sandra and froze. She couldn't believe what she was seeing and felt like driving her car into his to destroy them both. As she wasn't alone, there were innocent people with her who had nothing to do with what was happening, Celestina took a few deep breaths and got out of the car. Believe it or not, she was very calm and went straight up to him and said, "Tell your girlfriend to get out of the car right now."

Sandra got out with her head down and left; Celestina also turned her back on him, got into her car, and left.

The third lover, Amanda, was another work colleague of his; she also was married and living with her husband and children. She was different from the others because they were together five days a week at work, and there was no one else there, just them. It seemed she thought this gave her the right to call him at home whenever she wanted. Until one day, he left early in the morning and spent the whole day on the street, and Celestina was at home with the children. He got home very late and went straight up to the bedroom, and then the phone rang. Curious, Celestina picked up the phone and heard Amanda thanking him for the happy moments they'd had together. He heard Celestina pick up the phone and became agitated and shouted for Amanda to shut up, but it was too late. Celestina had heard, and right there on the phone she said, "Bitch, get off my phone, now!"

He calmed down and had the cheek to tell Celestina that he had the right to receive calls from his friends.

Celestina was so indignant that she called Amanda's house and left a message for her husband. The next day, Amanda told Rafael what Celestina had done, and he came into the house like a demon. He attacked Celestina mentally and physically, saying she was nothing, that he had made her what she was, he had put her where she was, and without him she was nothing. Celestina felt like a cockroach, and on top of that, Amanda called her and said she would take her to court for leaving that message at her home; she also threatened to smash her face in. Celestina told Rafael she couldn't stand it anymore, and he asked for forgiveness, for the first time in their entire relationship.

It was more than enough for Celestina. She came to understand why he had accused her of being Matheu's lover. It didn't matter how many apologies or pleas for forgiveness he asked of her, it was too late, because the love she felt for him had gone. Now she only felt rage and was afraid of what she might do. Celestina thought about lots of things, including doing bad things to him, but thanks to God, who was always by her side, she got rid of those bad thoughts. But Rafael had changed her into a cold and bitter person. At home, they didn't communicate; he did what he wanted, she did what she wanted, and they were married only on paper as they no longer shared anything else. Not even the bed, not because he didn't want to, because he kept insisting, with the same cynicism; she couldn't stand it anymore. She felt repugnance and disdain for him, but worse still, not just for him, but for any man.

Celestina knew that not all men were the same, but after a woman has lived with a man for so many years and suffered such horrible abuse, it's very hard to trust others. No kind of abuse is better than another. She had suffered from verbal, physical, emotional, and mental. The worst thing was the way he did it; he was a mentally ill, mean, and perverse person, who took pleasure in seeing her cry, to the point of destroying other innocent people. It was as if he planned everything he did to her down to the last detail, especially when the children weren't at home. She spent some of the most horrible times of her life with this demon.

Chapter 4

THE STRUGGLE FOR INDEPENDENCE

Celestina has cried, cried, and cried, many times. One day she was at home when Matheu came round to tell her about some problems he was having at work. Rafael wasn't home, but it wasn't long before he arrived. When he opened the door and saw the two friends talking on the couch, he didn't say a word; he just went straight to the laundry room, opened the dryer, and took out a handful of lint. He came back to the living room and, in front of Matheu, threw the lint at her head, saying, "Look how you've left the machine so dirty."

She was mortified and couldn't find any words to say; it was as if she was frozen and unable to move. Matheu understood what Rafael was trying to do, to embarrass her in front of him, so he said good-bye and left.

Another time, Celestina was propped up in bed and Rafael asked if she was sick. She said nothing, and he told her that her doctor had telephoned a few times, as he was worried about her. He also said that the doctor had told him that she had a contagious disease. When she heard this, she shouted like a madwoman, because this was not true. She tried to calm herself down and asked him who this doctor was, because she couldn't remember having been to see any doctor, what kind of illness this was, and why her results had been given to him and not personally to her. Rafael shut up and left. Shaking, she picked up the phone and called her doctor. She spoke to him directly and asked for an explanation of what was going on and what kind of contagious disease she had. The doctor replied that he had never called her house, nor had he spoken to Rafael at any time.

Celestina was terrified. She tried to understand how someone could be so perverse. Afterward, she was taken to the emergency room because her blood pressure had risen so high. Two days after she returned from hospital, she asked Rafael why he had lied, and he denied everything, saying he'd never said anything like that to her and suggesting that perhaps she had a dream.

On other occasions, when he saw it was almost time for her to go to work, he would start talking nonsense or complain about things from the past, and they would begin to argue. One day, she was so upset when she left that the police stopped her on the way to work, once for driving over the speed limit, another time for driving on the wrong side of the road, and a third time for going through a red light.

Sometimes Rafael came in from the street whistling; he sat down at the table to eat, and when he was done, he shouted the children's names and started talking crap. She had to leave the house to avoid fighting with him. Celestina waited until it was time for him to go to work and then came back. He was forever messing with her, saying that his family said he could find someone better and prettier than her. These things upset Celestina so much that she became bitter and, without wanting to think about the future or the present, considered ending her life. Usually when she returned home from work in the morning and saw his car parked in front of the house, tears ran down her face and her blood ran cold. When she opened the door, it was like being burnt by the fires of hell, scorching her soul with no way of stopping it. When the son of a bitch heard her coming in, he would come downstairs, and the same routine would begin.

She became so nervous that she stopped taking care of herself and began to eat, and eat, and eat. She ended up weighing over two hundred pounds. From wearing size 9 slacks, she started wearing size 14. She no longer had the will to live, and in her head, she wanted him to find her ugly, meet someone else, and disappear from her life forever. But he began to make fun of her, saying that she was very fat, ugly, and old. The more he insulted her, the more Celestina fell into depression. Sitting on the couch, eating and sleeping, she began to have problems walking, because her legs hurt so much from the weight and lack of exercise. She started losing her breath, taking a step or two and having to stop, so that her heart could catch up. With all this, she went on eating, as if the demon was pushing food into her mouth.

One day, Marta came to the house and saw her lying there like a piece of rotting meat, crying, with pains throughout her legs. She said to Celestina, "I am your sister and want what's best for you. I will not let this son of a bitch destroy you like this. You have to take control of your life, your children need you. Please, open your eyes, stop eating so much, get up off this couch, and start doing some exercise."

Celestina answered her, sobbing, "How can I walk, when I'm in so much pain?"

Marta suggested that Celestina take some Tylenol and wait a few minutes for it to take effect. Little by little, she started walking around the house and getting better day by day. She also started dancing. Rafael often tried to stop her from exercising. He would say that she was wasting time, that she wouldn't lose even a pound.

When he started doing this, she got angry and stopped exercising. Marta told her again not to let him get the better of her, and that is what she did. She stopped paying any attention to him, completely ignored his presence, and dedicated herself fully to her dancing. She danced for three or four hours straight every day and started to see some results. Then she decided to run in the street for an hour a day. The result was sensational; she lost thirty pounds in three months.

As she was still pretty fat, after two caesarians, her belly sagged so much that it covered her pelvis. She decided to have an operation to get rid of this extra skin and resolved to do it Brazil, because it was much cheaper and a friend of hers recommended a doctor there to Celestina. She arranged everything, flew to Brazil, had the operation, and returned.

She had a much smaller belly, but it didn't last long because the same problems began again. She started to get upset and to eat like before, and she got fatter than ever. She started feeling unwell, with lots of headaches, dizziness, and a heavy head, so she decided to see a doctor. He ran some tests for her cholesterol, glucose, heart, and head. When he got the results, he called her to come into the clinic.

When she got to the clinic, she was apprehensive; because something told her there was a serious problem. Her sugar and cholesterol levels were very high; the only good thing was that there was nothing wrong with her head. This doctor sent her to a heart specialist, who prescribed medication for her cholesterol; he also he banned her from eating sugar so she didn't become diabetic; she could only use sweetener. She had to take care of herself for her own good; as her sister had said, Rafael was to blame for all of this.

But God is greater than everything, and only he could enlighten her and show her the path she should take. She was very sad and down, so much so that she thought of taking her own life. She was tired of so much suffering and knew that she didn't deserve to live this way. When she saw people with happy marriages, she felt very angry and envious, because she wanted her own relationship to work. She wanted Rafael to treat her they way a woman should be treated. But there was no more hope, the love was over.

She no longer wanted to be in the same house as her husband, so she sought out a lawyer and was horrified at the price he wanted to charge for the divorce: $2,500! In addition, all the property, including her house, would have to be split up. If she wanted to continue living there after the divorce, she would have to give Rafael half the money that belonged to him, take out a bank loan, or sell the house; the poor children only had the right to 17 percent of his wages. She couldn't believe what the lawyer said. She told him that this was absurd; how could she take care of her children with so little money? And so there was no alternative, she stopped the divorce proceedings. Where would she find the money to pay the lawyer? How would her children eat and have clothes to wear? This was a desperate situation. What would become of their children in the future? There was not much hope for her; her life carried on worse than ever.

Then she thought back to something that had happened when she was just fifteen or sixteen. Her father had summoned her and two of her brothers to a meeting. He told them that he was going to divorce their mother because things were not going well between them. She was surprised because they hadn't seen them arguing or fighting. They always seemed like an exemplary couple. Her mother often told her that she always asked God to give her a husband like their father. When she asked why he wanted the divorce, her father had not given a clear explanation; she wanted to know what was really going on.

One day she sat down with her mother and started to ask questions. The answers were frightening, and she could hardly believe what she was hearing about her father. The reason he asked for a divorce was that he had a lover. Celestina almost passed out; how could he have the nerve to do such a thing? Her mother explained that her dad had had another woman for a long time. At the time, her mother was a hairdresser, and she told Celestina that he brought his lover to their house to have her hair done. What a lack of consideration!

But that wasn't all. One day, when they were all at home, her dad came into the house with a child in his arms. He told them that a lady who was crying in the street had given it to him, as she couldn't bring it up. They were happy; she was so small she seemed like a doll. Her mother wasn't too happy, but they pleaded and promised her that they would take care of this child, and they were all content.

But then one day, when her mother was looking through some documents, she found the child's birth certificate, which said that her husband, Celestina's father, was the child's legitimate father. Her mother almost died of a heart attack; the house became a hellish place, and it was never the same again. He took advantage of her mentally and morally in front of the whole family. How could he hurt her like that? She had considered this man an exemplary husband, the most respected on their street. But this secret was buried in the house, and her mom continued living with him, with the same respect as before.

At the time, she asked her mother why she didn't leave her father, and she replied that Celestina would understand when she was a mother one day. And it's so true! Nowadays she understands perfectly why she said that to her, although she reacted differently and tried to find help. But she knew that her independence, both emotional and financial, only depended on her, and she was getting there.

Chapter 5

INTERVIEWS ON DOMESTIC VIOLENCE

I feel quite angry that public appearance, most of the time, is false. Who do people think they're fooling? In my case, my husband and I fought at home, in the street, in the car, everywhere, and it was getting worse over time. That's why I decided to be open about my relationship with my work colleagues, because I'd always hidden the truth about my married life and the kind of person I was living with. In fact, people thought Rafael was the best man in the world, when it was all a big lie.

Why do we hide the abuses we suffer from boyfriends, fiancés, and husbands? I think it's because we're ashamed and always think one day they'll change and become the partner we so desire. Over time, I saw that was never going to happen; my anxiety and curiosity grew, and I started wondering how many other women there were with this problem. I started interviewing women on the street where I live, in the building where I work, everywhere I could, and the results were astounding! I learned a lot. I think I learned enough to talk about my problem and theirs.

The interviews are below; the first was one I did with a coworker from a few years ago.

Veronica

Veronica was very elegant and seemed very strong and secure. I confess that I was a bit envious of her when she talked about her relationship with Oscar, her husband: they took baths together, fed each other, and gave each other presents and flowers. I cried with envy inside and asked myself why I wasn't as fortunate as her. I kept this good image of her, and then we said good-bye after she changed jobs. The years passed, and one fine day, when I was at the supermarket, I saw Veronica. We were very happy to see each other. We talked for a good while, and I invited her out to lunch. She seemed very sad to me; her appearance and beauty were no longer the same, but she accepted my invitation, saying, "Let's, we have a lot to talk about."

At lunch, Veronica mentioned that she was having problems with two of her children, adolescent stuff, but she didn't think it was too serious. I asked about her love life, if it was the same as before, and confessed how I had been envious a few years ago. She smiled and then began to cry. I wondered if she had been widowed, but when she told me what had been going on, I would have preferred it if he were dead. She told me that Oscar often slapped her across the face. She said she was going crazy with the things he made her believe she had done.

One day when she wasn't feeling well, he gave her some medication. They were at the home of a family friend, and because of the medication, she fell asleep. When she woke up, Veronica found Oscar having sex with her friend! She wept bitterly, and I thought everything she told me was very serious. She said the guy was vermin, she was suffering a lot, he wasn't working, and she had been forced to give up their apartment due to lack of payment. Her children were going hungry.

She said that another friend who had been having marital problems gave her the telephone number of a social services agency where she could get help. She made an appointment that same day, and the lady who saw her was very moved by her story. She decided to talk to the children, and things got worse: they said that their father had threatened to kill everyone, chased them with a huge knife, and cut one of them on the leg (he still had the stitches). The police went to their house and all the locks were changed. Veronica took out an order of protection for her and the children.

When she was done explaining what had happened, we cried like children. I took her home, we said good-bye, and I asked her to take great care with him, adding that I'd keep in touch. A week later, I called Veronica because I was very worried about her situation. When I heard her voice, I knew she was a bit better and I was happy for her. But she told me that Oscar had asked for forgiveness several times, and she had forgiven him because he promised to change. He had come home and everything was going well. I was disappointed, but she told me she hoped he would get better, and I didn't want to tell her what I thought. Once again I told her to take care and hung up the phone. Years have passed, and my friend Veronica still lives in the hope that one day her husband will be the man all we women dream about.

Sarita

My second interview was with a woman who had known Rafael a long time before he met me. I worked with her a few years ago, but we weren't as close as we are now. Sarita seemed very sophisticated; she acted as though she was above everything and everyone. When we talked, she told me that Rafael seemed like a very good person. I said that I had lived with him for twenty-eight years and not even his own family knew him like I did. From that moment, it was as though a magic wand transformed Sarita; she no longer had that air of superiority and became fragile and suffering.

Sarita confessed to me that she also suffered from domestic violence. She told me that it was painful living with Daniel, her husband. He often threw hot milk into her face, burning her, and he made her go without food for days at a time. He would cook food for himself and then lock it up and take the keys to work. Often she would have to stay up and serve his friends through the night while they played cards. Sarita was often brought to her door by the police, as she was sleeping in her car. When Daniel started to beat her, Sarita ran out of the house and her car was her only refuge.

I ask myself if there were more people suffering this kind of abuse. If there were, I would like to listen, word for word, to what is happening to them.

Gimenia

I spoke with another work colleague, Gimenia, who seemed to be very sure of herself. How wrong I was! As soon as she opened her mouth, she started crying, and I shared her pain. When I listened to these women, it was like I was being stabbed in the heart.

Gimenia's husband Juan never allowed her to have a cell phone, and he always decided what they would eat every day. With tears in her eyes, she told me that sometimes she ate against her will, and when this happened, she would go to the bathroom and be sick. One day, he made her eat up all the vomit. I couldn't believe what I was hearing. I tried to comfort her, but we were both inconsolable. After a few moments of silence, I said I wasn't the best person to give her advice, but I thought she should look for help. She said that, in spite of everything, she loved Juan dearly.

After hearing about my conversation with Gimenia, other work colleagues started to talk to me with greater trust, because we all knew we weren't the only ones with this kind of problem. There is much, much more domestic violence than we thought. Imaculada asked me why we women suffer so much from our husbands, why they treat us so badly. I answered that our love for a man is sincere; this might be one reason, and another was our emotional or financial weakness.

Gimenia told me she had been married for a few years and couldn't stand it anymore, because her husband didn't want her to go to work. At the beginning of the relationship, she had been happy, but as time went on, she knew that something was wrong.

She couldn't go outside for anything, she had no friends, she never went to the store, and Juan locked her up at home twenty-four hours a day. I asked her why she didn't open the door and leave, she shouldn't stay against her own will. Gimenia replied, with tears in her eyes, that she wasn't the person she used to be, she didn't even have the strength to defend herself when he brutally forced her to have sex. Her life had changed, but she believed that some day it would get better. Everyone always thinks the same thing, that things will get better in the future. When?

Andrea

I also met Andrea in my line of work. She was a happy and very confident person; no one could imagine how much suffering was behind that smile. Andrea was also married, and her story was amazing. She said that her husband had never been diagnosed, but he was undoubtedly schizophrenic. She said this because she worked in a hospital for the mentally ill and saw Sam, her husband, as a sick man who needed help. Andrea told me that sometimes she was scared to death of him, and she hated coming home from work.

She also told me that he found something to argue about every day, accusing her of having sex with men from the street, claiming that so-and-so had said this or that, but in fact he was the one slandering her. He even told their friends that he was afraid of having sex with her in case he caught a sexually transmitted disease. She said that he begged her to go to bed with him, but she didn't want to because he was disrespectful to her and her children. A man who treats her with disdain, shames her in the eyes of others, flirts with the neighbors, and even thinks he's doing good, is an undignified, arrogant pig of a man.

Andrea told me she couldn't stand it anymore; she was terrified of him, and they hadn't slept together for many years. She knew he didn't have a woman on the street because he spent all his free time at home, making her life impossible. Besides being bad, the wretch was also mean, contributed nothing, and never bought enough food for the children. She worked like crazy to provide the best for her children. I told her she needed help, and decided to take her to an organization that defends women's rights.

Andrea spoke to someone at the organization, but when she came out of the office, she was weeping. I asked what had happened, and she said they couldn't help her because her children were not young enough and she wasn't being abused physically by her monster of her husband. I despaired when I listened to what she had to say, as she didn't have any marks on her indicating violence. This meant that she would have to be hurt physically to be able to receive any help.

What kind of world do we live in? This is why many women and children are murdered by their husbands or partners. I don't think there's much we can do. This situation leaves us with our hands and feet bound, and we have no way of finding help anywhere. It's as if all doors are closed, and we have to live with this situation for the rest of our lives. Everyone who is a victim of domestic violence is not there because they like being mistreated or they never sought help, but because they don't see a way out. I think the law, or the lack of it, allows the violence to continue. Psychological control is also a violent act; domestic violence is a crime like any other, and those who commit it should be punished.

Guadalupe

Guadalupe, a teacher, was married to Sebastian, a member of a well-respected family. The couple had two children who were also married with children. One day, Sebastian came home from work and handed his wife some documents, which he asked her to sign. Without thinking twice, Guadalupe unsuspectingly signed the documents. She didn't know she was voluntarily divorcing her husband and relinquishing all her rights to the marital property. They had spent more than thirty years together. She found out about the divorce in the newspaper; that day, she had a stroke and died.

Adriana

A childhood friend, Adriana, had a strong will and wanted to get on in life; she studied a lot and graduated from school. She looked for a good man to be her husband, as we all dream of, but our dreams don't always become a reality. Adriana fell deeply in love with Rodolfo and married him, and they had two children. Right from the start, he hurt her physically, but she kept hoping he'd change. We always hope they'll change, especially when they say, "See what you made me do? I didn't want to hit you, but you forced me to do this." It's what they all say, and we take the blame.

Every time they hurt us, deep down, we think things will get better, but the wretch makes life impossible. The lowlife didn't work; she took on all the responsibility, including all the expenses he incurred. Rodolfo forced Adriana to work overtime, and this money had to be deposited in the bank in both their names. She didn't have the right to take a dime. He also made her buy a car so he could work as a taxi driver, but this money was only for his personal expenses. Rodolfo had everything well thought out; he hired a divorce lawyer, got to keep the car and half the money in the bank. He took all his things from the house and disappeared as if the earth had swallowed him up. The worst thing is, Adriana does not want another man; she is waiting for him to come back to her. This life is full of mysteries and deluded people.

Marianita

Another friend, Marianita, who also lived in New York, has lived with domestic violence throughout her married life. It worsened day by day until her husband pushed her down the stairs; the police were called, and when they arrived, he was arrested and banned from entering the house. His brothers paid the bail and he stayed at one of their houses. After a few days, he asked her to take him back, because he missed his daughter, and promised that everything would be different. Stupid as ever, Marianita went to the police station to withdraw the charges she had brought against him. Even the officer who had arrested him was upset by this. We never learn that a leopard never changes its spots. What a mistake she made!

After a few days the violence began again; her husband, Kenne, said he wanted a divorce, and she fell into depression. One day, I was working and Marianita's daughter Bervale called me, saying that the police were at her house and her mother had tried to kill herself. I left work and went to her house, and there were two police cars outside. She had cut her wrist, and one of the police officers called me aside. He asked who I was and said he needed my help. I asked her what was going on, when she had cut herself and why.

Marianita replied that she no longer wanted to live, she couldn't take so much suffering, and she had cut herself at night. I told the policeman she had cut herself at night and asked why she hadn't gotten help sooner.

From what I understood, it didn't seem like Kenne wanted her to be helped; what he really wanted was for the policemen to send her for rehabilitation as if she were going crazy. And believe it or not, that's what happened. One of the policemen told me he needed my help, as he'd tried to take her to get help, but she'd refused. With tears in my eyes, I tried to explain to Marianita what could happen if she didn't agree to go with the officer; they'd have to take her by force. I told her not to worry, that I'd be with her for as long as it took, and everything would be fine. She agreed to go with the officer, and I followed them, and when I arrived at the hospital, she was already waiting for the doctor. She seemed very sad and kept on crying. Bervale and I tried to make her feel a bit better. When the psychologist arrived and called her in, the first thing she asked the attendant was whether she would be admitted to hospital. I asked if she wanted me to go with her, but with a smile she told me not to worry, she was fine, and she went in. Bervale and I sat in the waiting room. After about half an hour, Marianita emerged. I thanked God she wasn't going to be admitted, but the psychologist told her to come back, so she could get the help she needed. She promised she would change her behavior, but she fell into the lies once again and forgot her previous problems. I was stunned, but I couldn't do anything as, once again, she forgave her husband.

For a few months everything seemed to be going fine, but the problems continued, until one day Bervale turned up at my house, crying desperately and saying her parents were arguing. When I got to Marianita's house, she was crying because Kenne had punched her in the face. He had asked for a divorce, and as she hadn't expected it, she'd gone into shock. Deep down, not even I believed they would divorce. I tried to comfort her, saying that perhaps he would change his mind, and if not, she'd have to accept it and live her life normally, although that's easy for someone else to say; for her, it was impossible to live without him. She thought it was no more than a dream.

One afternoon, we were at her house talking when someone knocked at the door. When she opened it, there was a man with an envelope in his hand. He asked if the lady of the house was in and handed her the envelope, saying she had to appear in court. We were all surprised; we would never have imagined that the envelope contained divorce papers, sent by her husband's lawyer. Marianita, poor thing, fainted, and we all rushed around, not knowing what to do. After a few minutes she regained consciousness, crying and in despair. Oh God, what a sad day. After lots of crying, we calmed ourselves down and she went to sleep. The next day, she woke up much calmer, and as time went by, she seemed to be trying to accept the situation. It did not last long, and Bervale once again came to my house, saying that her mother wasn't feeling well, she was inconsolable after a crying fit, and I was worried about her.

From this moment on, everything changed. Marianita, once elegant, sophisticated, and good looking, became another person, losing all will to live, not caring about anything, and stopped taking baths, cooking, and looking after herself. To overcome all this, she chose a path that almost left her destitute, going to casinos and gambling to distract herself. She thought it was the only way to escape the depression, and without knowing it, she was falling into debt. Initially, she went with friends, perhaps once a month, then two to four times a month. I started getting worried and spoke to her, but her reply was, "Leave me alone, I need to have fun."

I told her that spending money like that wasn't fun and she should take care, because it was becoming a vice, but my advice was worthless because, instead of getting better, it got worse, and then some!

Then Marianita began missing work to go to the casino. I don't know how someone who doesn't work and doesn't get paid still gambles. I told her, please, think about what you're doing and spare a thought for your daughter, that this wasn't life, but it fell on deaf ears. I was losing my patience when I discovered that her vice was bankrupting her. We usually spent our holidays together, sometimes in another country, and in that damned year of 2007, she didn't show much interest in traveling. She made a lot of excuses, even saying she had a feeling that something was going to happen to the plane, but it was all an excuse, and I was about to find out why. A few days before buying the tickets, she received a check from her card, filled it in with the ticket amount, and gave it to me; I bought the tickets. I was quite happy, as I thought this problem was resolved.

A week later the agency called me and said the check had bounced due to lack of funds. I put my hands to my head, phoned Marianita, and told her what had happened. Her answer left me speechless; she had put $11,000 on her card to play at the casino. I asked if she was crazy and, for the love of God, to open her eyes, because this was very serious. I ended up having to pay for the tickets, as I didn't want to go and leave her here alone. I did the impossible, working overtime to give her money for her expenses, and once again, she did hers. Every week I tightened my belt to save a bit of money, which I kept in the house, but something told me I should go and check it, and when I opened the envelope, there was $300 missing. It was then I really knew that she had a very serious problem.

Shaking, I phoned Marianita, because I wanted to know what she had done with the money I was keeping. She told me she had taken it to make a payment of hers, but I was not satisfied with the response, as I was absolutely certain she'd taken the money to gamble at the casino. I was very disappointed when I saw how this addiction had taken over her, and she didn't care how or where she got the money to gamble from. But not even this stopped me from working to save the holiday money, or letting her go. We traveled for the vacation, and I felt her begin to change; first of all, she no longer gambled as she had done before and she started going to church a lot. When we returned home, she seemed like another person; she began cooking again, washing clothes, cleaning the house, and best of all, she recognized the error of her ways, spending money on gambling. She told me that she couldn't understand why she'd done what she'd done, that never again in her life would she go to a casino. God is so wonderful!

She is now much better, and her depression is under control. We must pray a lot for God to give her much peace, health, and tranquility, and have a great deal of faith in her. I don't know what will happen to my friend after the problem I've just described, but for now she is taking a bit more responsibility and is more disciplined, paying her bills alone, as Kenne continues on as before. She went back to him. Who are we to judge her? Even knowing everything that happened was his fault. She's still in love like the first day, and we all know that love doesn't put food on the table or pay the bills. That's why these cases often end in tragedy.

Juanita

Another acquaintance of mine suffers from domestic violence. Juanita was tall, pretty, and very elegant, and then she met a man who began pushing her around before they were married. She kept quiet and never told anyone what was happening. Roberto, her husband, was very hardworking and always treated everyone else well, but on the other hand, he was violent toward her. One day, after they had been married a few months, she called her mother to come and help her, because Roberto was beating her. Her mother became very agitated by the news and couldn't go and see her, so she sent Maria, her other daughter, to find out what was going on.

When Maria say Juanita, her sister's arm was all bloody; Roberto had beaten her in front of their small child, and she had tried to defend herself, but he had bitten her arm and almost taken a chunk out. Maria called him a coward and tried to console her sister. From there on, things got worse; he kept hitting her in front of the children, and then something else serious happened. He came in from the street and started to argue with her, but as she ignored him, he grabbed her, took her into the bedroom, threw her on the bed, put a pillow over her head, and started to punch her in the face, with their helpless son shouting and crying for his mother. This is how their five children grew up, seeing everything their father did to their mother. Then one day the eldest son couldn't bear his mother crying and yelling from the pain of the endless punches dished out by his father; he decided to face his father and tell him to stop hurting his mother. Things got ugly, and Roberto furiously turned against the son, trying to hit him, but, thank goodness, things settled down. Juanita asked her son, for the love of God, not to get involved when he heard the fights so as not to create more problems. From that day on, whatever happened, they stayed still, listening and crying, until everything returned to normal, seeing their mother all bruised and unable to walk. The fights continued; by day everything was fine, but when night came, everyone got frightened whenever they heard a noise and ran to hide from their own father.

One morning, Juanita was putting out clothes on the roof with her grandson, when she suddenly started to feel pain in her chest. Everything went dark, and she woke up in the hospital, all twisted. She'd had a stroke. Who's to blame for this? She spent several days in the hospital; the doctors were very concerned about her condition and demanded absolute rest and that, under no circumstances, could she get upset. To prevent this from happening, Maria took her home to take care of her. With all the patience in the world, she carefully gave her medication at the right times, bathed her, fed her, and took her to her doctor's appointments; she stayed there for months, and her recovery went well. The time came to face reality, to return home with her husband and children. When she got home, everyone was waiting for her with open arms, anxious not to upset her so she would get better as quickly as possible.

After this, everything was going well at home, but things never returned to normal; she'll never be the same again.

Anna

This case is very sad for me because it is about Anna, my friend's niece. Anna was born and raised in Brazil. She is so young and has suffered so much. I had already left Brazil to come and live in New York when she was born, and whenever I went back to Brazil to visit my family,

I watched her grow from a baby to an adult woman. Anna was always a wonderful girl in every sense, sweet, sentimental, kind, polite, and intelligent. A person like that deserves a partner who loves her in the best possible way. Why do we women settle for so little? It hurt a lot, seeing how she was brought up, with so much love and care, not only from her parents, but from all the other members of her family, and everyone suffered when they knew about her suffering.

Anna met Juan, and they started dating, but they didn't take the time to get to know each other better before they moved in together. She rented an apartment and arranged everything, something he should have done. As far as her parents were concerned, everything was going well, but some members of the family knew that things between them were not good; one day her aunt was at home and heard an argument. She went down to find out what was going on and found Juan shouting, looking like he was about to hit her. When the aunt intervened, he said she shouldn't get involved and threatened her with a gun, as if he owned her and the house too. But Anna's uncle intervened, and Juan went away. It was then Anna realized she had serious problems with this man, but she didn't tell them.

Over time, everyone forgot what had happened, and everything went back to normal, but I always thought Juan was devious. He always kept his mouth shut in front of the family, but when they weren't there he took off his mask. It didn't take long for the bomb to explode. One day when everyone was gathered for Easter, they called me, and from their tone of voice, I knew something serious was going on. Anna had gotten tired of paying for him, buying food, clothes, making all the payments, and giving him money for his expenses. Besides that, he even controlled all her money in the bank.

One day, Juan went to withdraw her money from the bank, but he found nothing there. By now Anna had realized the kind of good-for-nothing he was, so she had withdrawn the money in advance. When he found there was no money, he went mad and went looking for her, shouting that she had withdrawn his money and he wanted it back. How is it that he didn't work but wanted money in the bank? Things got so ugly that the police had to intervene, but he continued demanding his money and even threatened to kill her.

This is what happens when we give men the good life. Deep, deep down, women are to blame for many of the things that happen. We shouldn't keep it secret when we suffer from domestic violence, but most women think their partners will change, which isn't true because, generally, people don't change. My friend told me, "Men don't change, it's us women who change," and that's why the problems occur. She said that when we're married, and doing everything they want, the relationship is fine, but when we get tired, because we're disappointed, the purest and most sincere love we felt is extinguished because we no longer have the hope that they will get better.

This is exactly what happened to Anna. She was already preparing to be independent, and when the family found out about everything, they started to protect her. After the scandal Juan had caused and many others, her parents were afraid to let her go home with him. She moved back with them, and he continued threatening her; he even demanded that she should pay for the apartment, which had been rented in her name. Juan refused to move out and continued living there after she left.

Anna's life became a living hell; she had to leave college because she couldn't pay for it; she owed thousands of dollars in student loans. The worst thing was that she became a very sad and quiet girl, not because she was like that, but because she was suffering so much. Everyone in the family was worried; every night her father waited for her at the bus stop when she came home from work.

But thank God, little by little, things returned to normal. God enlightened her so that she returned to her religion, and with her faith, she is now a completely different person. She's paid all her debts, she helps her parents financially, dresses very well, and lives happily. She won this battle.

Eleventh Interview

Carlos and Rosa lived happily together with their daughter, but over the years, they no longer understood one another. They always ended up arguing, and one day, Rosa had to call the police because Carlos threatened to destroy everything in the house. The police talked to him and things went back to normal. After a few days, the same problem happened again. This time was much worse, however, because he pushed Rosa down the stairs and broke the dining room table. She ran to the neighbor's house, crying, afraid that he would do something worse to her. After a few minutes, everything returned back to normal, but when she got home, her panties were all in the trash, all cut up, especially around the private parts.

This was not the first time her panties had gone missing. Every time they had a problem at home, Carlos took a knife and cut up her panties in a rage, as if he was doing it to her. Despite this, Rosa didn't take it seriously; it wasn't a big thing for her at the time, but her neighbor told her to be careful with him, because he seemed ill, schizophrenic, and you never knew what he might do the next time a problem occurred. For a few days, the husband remained calm, and she looked happy! She thought that this time, he was making an effort to make it work.

But it was all in vain, as one night, when Rosa was sleeping, she heard a noise in the room, and when she lifted her head, she saw Carlos at the panties drawer. She pretended to be asleep, and when he left the room and went downstairs, she stayed in bed, seeing what he would do. She heard an odd sound, he seemed like a rabid dog, murmuring and cutting the panties with a knife. After a few seconds, everything went quiet; she went downstairs and saw that he had left. To be sure of what he'd done, she went to look in the trash, and there were her panties, covered in blood! She thought he must have cut himself stabbing them.

The next day, he returned and told her that he needed a vacation, and she agreed, as he didn't seem at all well. He bought a ticket and went to his home country, Santo Domingo. His attitude showed that he really thought he'd stabbed someone to death and was running from justice.

He stayed there for over three weeks, as it seemed that he thought his supposed crime of the panties was forgotten.

When Carlos returned from his trip, he was a bit calmer and much more loving. Of course, we all know why: he wanted to have sex with her again, and stupidly, she accepted. Oh, what is love? But Rosa didn't know what was about to happen. Her husband had brought back a black stone; he told her she had to wet it a bit with her tongue and then put it on her genitals and have sex with him. She was very happy; she fell into his arms passionately, but after a few minutes of penetration, got out of bed naked, shouting, in great pain with a burning sensation in her vagina. Unable to bear the pain, she put on a nightdress and ran outdoors, with the cold and all, feeling as if everything was about to come out from inside of her; even her nose was bleeding. When she went to get a towel from the bathroom to clean her nose, she felt something running down her legs and saw that it was blood. Panicking, and covered in blood, she started shouting, putting her hands on her body and on the bathroom walls, making them dirty. It was a very sad scene! The neighbor still doesn't understand what happened, because she said he asked for forgiveness, saying it wasn't intentional, and she believed him, and she forgave him!

Nowadays, Rosa lives on medication, to get a bit of peace, but stays with Carlos and the problems, as before. Her panties continue to disappear and are always found in the trash, all cut up. Her neighbor, concerned, always asks her what his intentions really are and prays to God to take care of her and of her daughter.

Chapter 6

CASES OF VIOLENCE AGAINST WOMEN THROUGHOUT THE WORLD

After I started talking to women about domestic violence, I found that this was a frequent situation in many homes. I decided to write down cases of violence that were made public by the media and to research the subject on the Internet. Some of these cases appeared on American television. Below I have transcribed some of the first cases I noted down that horrified me the most about domestic violence, because I saw that society consents to violence. They made me research many more cases, that I have separated into specific chapters later on.

Africa

Girls of eight to ten years were handed by their parents to the parents of their future husbands so they could learn everything that was needed to be a good mother, and after they were prepared and were menstruating, it was time for their marriage. They were handed to their husbands and when they became pregnant, there was no hospital for the birth; they gave birth at home, alone, and far from everything and everyone. They screamed for hours and hours with the labor pains, with no one to help, and the pain was such that, in despair, they cut their genitals themselves so the babies could be born. Often the babies were born dead, and these adolescent mothers continued without any medical assistance. After a while, their bodies were like that of a child; they were not ready to give birth, and uncared for, they started to go downhill, with an unpleasant smell. Their husbands often returned them to their parents. With the shame of their returned daughters, their parents would build a small room at the back of the house and leave them there in isolation, because of the comments from the neighbors, where they stay until they die. A couple of American doctors chose this African country to vacation in and found out what happens with these children. Without thinking about what they left behind, the two decided to set up a small place to cure these children, and that was how everything began. Many of these children traveled or walked for many days to get to their clinic, where the injuries they sustained giving birth were operated on. Sometimes, some of them died, unable to bear the pain due to serious infection. The doctors continue to live there and never came back to their country.

Brazil

Another case happened in Brazil. A man and woman were married for twenty years. People used to talk about how close they were; there was a lot of love, passion, understanding, and trust between them. But one day there was a big problem; the husband became jealous after he found out his wife was having an affair with another man. He waited until she went to sleep, and then he boiled a pot of water and threw it all over her face. It wasn't until after he was already in prison, paying the crime, that he learned that his wife wasn't having an affair.

United States of America

One of the cases I saw was of a husband who strangled his wife whilst she slept, saying that women were born to be slaves. Another verbally abused his wife every day, demanding that she give him a bath and put food in his mouth. Some say women are only good to cook, wash, and iron, that they shouldn't work so that they don't get to meet different people and can't have any of their own money. Some order them to not have a bath until they get home to check their private parts, to know whether they have had sex with another man. Generally, the husband thinks the wife is his property and has no rights, not even to drive without his approval, and control her twenty-four hours a day. He demands that they weigh themselves two or three times a week, and if they are over a certain weight stipulated by him, he does not allow her to eat until her weight falls. Another husband said that women are born without a brain and that God made men to use and abuse women. One man said that his wife was made to have children, to take care of the house, and to make love to him whenever he wanted it.

When I heard this on the TV, I was very angry with myself because, a few years back, I found myself this situation. I didn't go anywhere without Rafael, who also thought me an ignorant person and often said that I was good for nothing. I was also forbidden from having friendships with colleagues where I worked and with my family. He made me feel ashamed of myself in front of everyone. One example: a few years ago, a carpenter was working in our house and we were talking. Rafael came in and started shouting, saying he had been listening to us and that people were talking about him, saying that I was going out with the carpenter. There were many other bad moments, but they were so unpleasant I prefer not to remember them.

In Los Angeles, there was a married lady who always separated from her husband whenever she suffered from his violence. Unable to take anymore, she decided to leave him for good. In trying to rebuild her life with a new love, the same thing happened: she was hurt emotionally and physically by her new man, and he also tried to abuse and kill her small daughter. She is now undergoing rehabilitation with clinical help.

In another case, a husband became jealous of his wife over nothing, and one day he got home and started to beat her. Desperately, she ran out and got in her car, and he started throwing gas over the car. Terrified, she got out of the car, and he threw gas over her and lit a match, setting her on fire. Now her body is deformed.

Another rogue, thinking that his wife was cheating on him, threw acid over half of her body.

Another similar case happened here in New York. As the woman was asking for a divorce for reasons of abuse, the husband swore she would not go off with another man. He waited in hiding for her to get home from work, and when he heard her coming upstairs, he came out and threw acid over her face.

Also in New York, there was a couple who had divorced. The man came into the house and started stabbing his ex-wife, and when he saw she was no longer moving, he ran away. She dragged herself to the telephone and called for help.

One more case: A woman was married but it didn't work out. He beat not only her but the children as well, as if they were animals. But one day, he found a girlfriend, and on the spur of the moment, he disappeared. No one missed him in the family; she went on working and taking care of her children, alone. After a year and a half, he returned, as always without work, and told her that if she didn't take him back he would kill her. The poor thing was advised to leave the country and try to make a new life somewhere else with her children and bring charges against him as quickly as possible, as he was very dangerous.

India

In this country, parents often choose husbands and wives for their children; every family wants to ensure the future of their off spring. Parents who hand over their daughter have the obligation to provide their future in-laws with expensive presents or gold to obtain their affection. As far as I am concerned, this custom is outrageous, as the women are negotiated with as if they were objects in the marriage, and if some day, for any reason, they are unable to continue giving presents to their in-laws, things change, and the husbands burn their bodies, principally the face, and their small daughters too if they try to defend the mothers.

Peru

In Lima, the capital of Peru, one man obliged his wife to send their children to an orphanage, forced her to have sex with him in front of the children, and often disappeared for days; when he returned, he beat her. On top of all this, he had four lovers, the first of which he obliged to have two abortions; another became pregnant; one was just sixteen years old; and one was a homosexual cousin of theirs.

In another case, a wife was left mute after she was stabbed by her husband in the throat. In another, a married woman had two children. Her husband threw their son out of the house when he was just eight years old, and the poor thing had to sleep on the street. The husband beat their daughter and tried to drown her, and then he attacked his wife when she tried to defend the daughter. She was stabbed all over her body.

Another case took place in Lima; a married man managed to get a girlfriend by telling her that he was single. After a few months together, she became pregnant, and as always happens with men, he denied he was the father of the child. One day, he took her to a mental hospital and made her throw herself off the building to lose the child. She ended up in hospital as a result

El Salvador

One husband frequently used physical violence against his wife, and one day he used an axe on her head, wounding her in the shape of a cross; he also cut her hands, which were left hanging by the skin. She now uses a wheelchair, is mute, and is paralyzed by an axe blow to her back. The man is untouched as if he had done nothing.

I also examined some brief cases of women who made a fresh start after their first failed marriage and started another relationship. As always, the children are the ones who suffer most.

One woman from Lima, who had separated from her husband and was raising their three children, met another guy and started to trust him. But in this case the abuse was even worse, due to her fear of being alone again. One day she went out, leaving him alone in the house with her children, and when she returned, she found him raping her eight-year-old daughter. Crazy from anger at seeing what was happening, she didn't think twice, took a knife, and stabbed the rogue many times, until she was sure he was dead. She was arrested but was not held for long, because her man had also abused her seven-year-old son and was threatening to kill him.

In another case, a mother sent her ten-year-old daughter out of the house to work as a prostitute, for her own upkeep and that of her second husband. Another mother sent her fifteen-year-old daughters out of the house, fearing that they would take her husband, saying that she would rather throw her daughter out so that she wouldn't lose her man. In another example, after being abandoned by her husband, a mother turned against her daughter and made her a slave in the house, forcing her to do everything, and the poor thing got tired of this and ran away because she was being abused sexually by her stepfather. We should never trust our children with any man.

Chapter 7

CASES OF WOMEN MURDERED BY THEIR MEN

After enduring humiliating verbal, emotional, and physical aggression and lack of support from the authorities, all we women can expect for certain is death. So that my readers know how women are dying throughout the world, I will tell you about some of the cases I found about through the media. Husbands often kill their wives because of anger, jealousy, possessiveness, financial difficulties, child custody, or because they didn't want to pay child support, but what really leaves me astounded is that often the reasons are so trivial, such as wanting to watch a favorite program on the TV or because the food is not hot.

United States of America

Arizona

1. This case involved an elderly couple, he was eighty-two years old and she was eighty. He arrived home and started arguing with his wife for no reason, saying he would kill her. Very afraid, she called the police and said that her husband wanted to kill her. The police did not arrive, and he went downstairs with a rifle in his hands and sat on the couch; she very calmly asked him not to kill her, but he pulled the trigger and then called the police, saying he had killed his wife. When the police finally arrived, he tried to make out that it was an accident. He was charged and convicted, and he died a few years later in prison.

2. There was a couple who lived in Phoenix and had a swimming pool in the yard; all the neighbors knew them as a friendly and loving couple. One evening, the wife asked her husband to fix a problem with the swimming pool, and he went to see what it was. After a few minutes, he returned, saying it was too dark outside and promising her he would fix it the next day. Later that night, while their children were sleeping peacefully, he went to the garage, where he changed clothes, putting on jeans and a shirt, took a knife, and stabbed his wife, who had gone swimming in the pool. He returned to the swimming pool and found his wife still breathing. One of the neighbors saw him pushing her into the swimming pool, holding her head under the water. The neighbor called the police, and when they arrived, they found him covered with blood. The excuse he gave was that he was sleepwalking; he had no idea what had happened. He was convicted and given a life sentence.

California

1. A bride was murdered on her wedding day by her ex-boyfriend. Everyone was at home, preparing for the wedding, when he turned up with a revolver and started shooting. Everyone ran, but the bride was unlucky, shot down dead in her white dress, all covered in blood.

2. Another lady broke up with her fiancé because she couldn't take his abuse any more. When she went to work in her beauty parlor, he arrived, pulled out the revolver, and shot her, saying that if he couldn't have her, nobody could. She tried to defend herself, even calling 911, the police emergency number, but by the time they got there it was too late. She was already dead.

3. A young man was looking for a wife; he went to a friend's wedding, where he met a girl who was also looking for her Prince Charming. They started talking and were the last to

leave the reception. They understood each other so well that they continued dating. One day, she took him to meet her parents, but they were not very happy because he was in such a rush to marry. However, as their daughter was keen, they gave their consent. After they got married, he brought her to their home, which was in a remote location. When she got there, she had her first surprise: it was the only house around. But love is blind, and she was very much in love.

One day her parents decided to go pay her a surprise visit. When they arrived, they were not very well received by her husband. When she saw this, they started to argue, and he asked if he could be alone with her for a few minutes. He took her horse riding. This was the last time the parents saw their daughter alive, as she never returned. He pulled her from the horse, took a stone, and hit her on the head and then injected her with a fatal dose of phenobarbital.

4. A husband accused his wife of sleeping with lots of men and also said that she was a bad example to their children. But her neighbors thought differently; as far as they were concerned his wife was very devoted to their children, but this didn't stop the husband, who killed her with a bullet to the heart.

5. A woman decided to divorce her husband, as there were many problems between them. When he found her with another man, without thinking twice he shot her in the head along with her companion. He lost his memory for a while, but she was not so lucky and died in hospital hours after his confession, in which he said he couldn't stand seeing his ex in the arms of another.

6. I don't know why we women are so naive. A woman was married and lived in a comfortable situation financially, and the two of them loved each other madly, but her husband had an accident and died. He left her well off, with $2 million, with which she could live the rest of her life without any problem. A few years later, she started dating a man who had

been around since the day her husband died. They began to go out and became engaged. But her mother didn't think that she should marry this man. As always, we don't accept advice because as the saying goes, "If advice was good, it wouldn't be given away, it would be sold." She didn't listen to her mother and married the guy. They moved to California, where they bought a big house, and he brought along a friend of his to help with the move. Everything seemed to be going well until one day she discovered her husband was spending her money, going to parties with friends, and taking money from her account and putting it into a separate account for him. Worried and disappointed, she confronted him about this and they began arguing. He took a heavy object and hit her on the head so hard that it killed her. He and his friend took her body and put it in the car; the friend drove away but had a big accident. He ended up in hospital. A few days later the friend disappeared from the hospital, but later he was found and ended up confessing that he and the husband had planned the crime. They were tried and convicted.

7. A young woman aged twenty or so years was pregnant and disappeared days before she was due to give birth, when she was out shopping for the baby with her five-year-old son. Her sister thought it was her boyfriend, a married man who already had one child. They were always fighting and he didn't want to do anything for the child she was expecting. After two months of searching, the sister received a phone call, saying they had found an unidentifiable body floating in a lake. No one knows what happened to the unborn child or the five-year-old son who was with her on the day she disappeared. To this day no answer has been found and there has been no clue either as to the whereabouts of the murderer who committed this brutal crime.

8. A beautiful, intelligent seventeen-year-old girl was a talented ballet dancer. She danced like a professional, and her teachers thought she would go far with her talent, but unfortunately she met an older man who did everything she wanted. As time

passed, he thought she was becoming more distant from him and told her that she was wasting her time dancing. He asked her to stop dancing, and she answered that she loved him, but she loved dancing much more. He took a knife and stabbed her many times, killing her. He was arrested and convicted of the crime.

9. In Hollywood, a nineteen-year-old had a child with her boyfriend, and they lived together in an apartment. Mothers always know what's best for their children, and her mother always told her that this man wasn't good for her; he was very strange, aggressive, and rude. One day, after she fell asleep with the child on the couch, he tried to take the boy. When she woke up and saw what he was doing, she fought him tooth and nail to get her child back. The boyfriend, in a fit of fury, started to beat her all over her body, but mainly on her face and head, killing her, and then he took the child and disappeared. The mother and her brothers hope that someday the police will find their grandchild and nephew, and that one day they will catch the murderer so he can pay for the crime he committed.

10. Every day when I open a newspaper or watch television, I feel depressed and ask myself what is happening, not just here in the United States, but everywhere in the world. Domestic violence is growing at an alarming rate. I ask myself too what makes someone commit crimes in a family. Mental illness? Uncontrollable emotions? Despair? Depression? In Los Angeles, a man lived with his wife and three children and was violent at home, but no one could have imagined that the problem was so serious. One morning, when everyone was at church, this man took his revolver and killed his wife's grandparents and her cousin. The wife was already dead in the apartment, and the police arrested him when he was carrying one of the children, but all the children were saved.

North Carolina

1. In a small town where everyone knew each other, a man fell in love with a young girl who came from a good family, had many good attributes, and dreamed of the big life one day. The two didn't think of the consequences of what might happen in the future, but their parents and friends did, because she was black and he was white. As they were very much in love, they decided to get married and move to California. Everything was fine until he decided to visit some places where black people couldn't get in and neither could he, because he was married to a black woman. It was then that the abuse started. One day the doorbell rang; she looked through the window and saw a beautiful bunch of roses. When she opened the door, the delivery man shot her in the chest, and she fell down dead right there. Her husband had paid someone to kill her, because it was the only way he would be able to visit the places of the whites and the famous. The worst of it is, that to this day, the guy has still not paid for his crime.

2. A couple had three children, two boys and a girl. Everything seemed to be going well; he seemed like a very romantic person, the type who likes to have candles around the bathtub with a few drinks, but one day he found his wife dead in the bathtub. The ambulance and police arrived, and at the end of the investigation, it was declared a case of accidental death. Sometime later, this man claimed his wife's life insurance and decided to move to another state with his children, in search of a new wife to be mother for the children. With the insurance money, he bought a big house, and it was not long before he met someone. Very happy, he took her to meet the children, and they decided to get married. He began again with the fun times in the bath with candles and drinks, and then what happened? She was also found dead in the bathtub. His excuse this time was that he had left her alone when he heard a noise, and when he returned, she was dead. What a coincidence, the two of them died in the same way and from the same cause. This drew the attention of the authorities,

and they started to investigate further and discovered that it was not an accident. He had suffocated her and put her head down in the bathtub, as if she had drowned. To everyone's surprise, his first wife had also been murdered by him in the same way. He is in prison, paying for his crimes, but none of his three children believe that he killed their mother or stepmother.

3. Two nurses left the hospital where they worked together to have lunch, and as they drove back to work, the one who was driving was shot. She was a married woman, with two children and an excellent husband who worked for the fire department; he was seen as an exemplary man. The passenger was a single woman with two children, who had a very aggressive boyfriend. When she saw her friend had been shot, she got out of the car and was also shot. When help arrived, the two women were taken to hospital, but the driver died on the way. The husband of the one who was driving was told that his wife had been killed. When he heard this news, he became so upset that he punched the wall and broke his hand. The boyfriend of the passenger was also called and told that she was in critical condition. He cried a lot but had no problem cooperating with the police. A few days later, the husband of the driver called the police, saying that someone had tried to kill him, and after a lot of investigation, they found that he was in debt and unable to pay what he owed. He decided to confess that he hadn't wanted to kill his wife, he had only wanted to frighten her, and that it was all an accident. He was tried and given a life sentence.

4. A man brutally murdered his eighteen-year-old wife. His friends told him that she was cheating on him, so he took a knife and stabbed her seventy-two times, leaving her dead in the house. He is now in prison, paying for his crime.

5. A woman who suffered from her husband's violence every day decided to leave their home in Florida and go to her summer house in North Carolina. When he found out that she had

left home, he talked to their neighbors, and they arranged to murder the poor woman. The couple left Florida for North Carolina with everything planned; he even gave them the key to the house. When they got there, they waited for the woman to go to sleep, entered the house, and beat her to death. Then they put her body in her car, drove it to a deserted place, and let the car roll down a steep slope, as if it were an accident. The reason for the murder was $100,000 life insurance, which the husband promised to pay half to the couple who committed the crime. The three of them are paying for their crimes with a life sentence.

6.   For me, this is a very sad case because I feel the pain of this mother. We always say that our children are supposed to bury us, but it doesn't always happen this way, especially when it is not a natural death. A work colleague received the news that her daughter's boyfriend had murdered her with eight shots in the back and then shot himself in the head, trying to kill himself, but he survived. The worst of it is that the daughter left two children, one eight years old and the other just a few months old; the children witnessed everything.

South Carolina

1.   The police and fire department were called to put out a fire that appeared in the middle of the street, and when they had finished, they found the body of a woman, who had received many blows to the head. The woman's husband had reported her as missing, with their newly born daughter. It took six years of investigation to discover that the murderer was the husband himself. He confessed his crime and will pay for it in prison.

2.   In Manchester, a heartless man threw a roofing tile from the top of his house onto his wife's head, sending her to hospital, but he wasn't successful in doing what he wanted, which was to kill her. Not satisfied with the result, after seeing his wife

completely recovered, he tried one more time. When the woman left to take the dog for a walk, he shot her several times in the back, leaving her dead body spread out across the ground. Justice was done, and he was sentenced to life imprisonment.

Colorado

1. There was a couple who were a model for the community, and there was no sign of any kind of domestic violence between them. But one day her husband called the police to report that his wife had disappeared and asked for help in finding her. Immediately, the police started to investigate and found letters in the house and phone calls from him to another woman, who was none other than his sister-in-law, his own brother's wife. This was the reason he had killed his wife; his son, who was just a few months old, witnessed everything. He placed her body in the car and left it in a deserted place. As always happens in these cases, days before the murder, he had taken out half a million dollars in life insurance in the wife's name, thinking he would start a new life with the sister-in-law, because he was very much in love with her. He was tried and sentenced to life in prison, but the sister-in-law is still in touch with him.

2. In Denver, a married couple had a friend who lived with them; the friend told the police that from time to time they fought violently. One day, the wife's body was found, unrecognizable; it could only be identified by her fingerprints. Her body had been dragged behind the car for more than a mile. In the autopsy, they found that she had suffered injuries to the head and had been strangled. The husband is in prison awaiting trial.

Connecticut

Day by day, domestic violence is on the increase; for all kinds of reasons, however minor, a woman can be in danger at the hands of a man. In one case, a man was offended because his girlfriend broke off with him, and in revenge, he stabbed her many times and killed her. He turned himself in to the police and will pay for his crime.

Florida

1. A doctor fell in love with his nurse, and without knowing each other well, he went to her parents' house to get to know the whole family. As mothers can always sense when things are not good for their children, from the first day she met him, her mother felt he was not the right man for her daughter, but as the rest of the family approved, she didn't have much choice and accepted him, and after a few months they were married. Everything seemed to be going well until she went to her youngest sister's house, who saw that her face was all black from the punches he had given her. The sister asked her what had happened and she gave an unconvincing excuse; worried, the sister told her husband what she was thinking, but he convinced her that everything was fine.

   One day, the nurse showed up at her parents' house, and this time she didn't want to leave the car; she decided to leave, and this was the last time her family saw her alive. When she got home, the monster of her husband was waiting for her and had everything planned. They began to argue, and using his exercise equipment, he deformed the whole of her body with many blows, and threw her body on the highway, where it was found by a passerby.

2. A couple who had been married many years decided to get a divorce, and the wife was given custody of the children. After some time, she met a young man and they started dating. As men only value their wives after they lose them, dying of

jealousy, the ex-husband began to prowl round her house, watching over her. The worst happened, but it is not known whether he killed her himself or if he paid someone to kill her in the worst possible way.

3.　There was a couple with three boys who seemed like the ideal family. They had their own house, she dedicated herself to looking after their children, and everyone lived happily, or so it seemed. Behind the façade, he was a womanizer who loved to party; he spent many nights in casinos with his lover and friends, and when he returned home, he was an authoritarian. The good thing was the mother was really close to her children, and this helped her to keep leading that life. One day, her husband arrived home from work and agreed with his wife that they would spend the weekend in a casino, which she accepted just to please him, as she didn't gamble. Innocently, she was unaware that he already had everything planned for her death. He had hire someone to kill his wife, and they arranged to follow his car; when he pulled over into a rest area, pretending that something was wrong with the car, one of the guys would come up and shoot her. With a single bullet in her chest she was shot dead and the murderers disappeared.

4.　Another case that touched the whole of New York involved two young people who met in the restaurant where he worked; both of them were from good families and were studying at college. The two started dating, and he met her family, and they were very satisfied with their daughter's future, and his family also accepted her. The couple were very happy and decided that after they graduated they would marry. They had a beautiful wedding ceremony, and after their honeymoon, they decided to open a small restaurant. Business was good, and then he decided to start a new life in Florida, using the money from the sale of the business to buy a house, and everything was just great. After a short while, they announced that they were expecting a child, and everyone was very happy at the news and started making plans for the next member of the family. However, the husband had a lover, and with a child on the way, he perhaps thought he would lose the lover.

It was then that he committed the worst monstrosity in the world. It was Christmas Eve when the whole of New York heard on the television that a pregnant woman went out to walk her dog and disappeared. When I heard this, I wondered why her husband had let his pregnant wife go out alone with the dog; why didn't he go with her? And when he gave an interview to a reporter, he acted so coldly, saying that he knew his wife was alive, that he would keep the house just as it was for when she returned. He wanted to get his lover to lie for him, he wanted to sell the house, and with all this, her family still couldn't believe that he had anything to do with her disappearance. The lover decided to tell the police everything she knew. The husband then changed the color of his hair, took his brother's ID, and tried to disappear, but he was found and arrested by the police. How he killed his wife and their unborn child remains a mystery. Their bodies were found not very far from the place where he always went fishing. They found her body first, then the child's body in the sea.

5. A policeman stopped in a cantina to have a coffee and met a young woman who was much younger than him. He started to flirt with her, and after he had seen her two or three times, she started dating him (she did not know he was married). At the start, everything went just fine, but afterward the abuse started because of the jealousy that was gnawing away at him. The young lady was very pretty, and soon she started seeing another young policeman, a colleague of his. He couldn't take his defeat. When he met her on her way back from work, he stopped the car and offered her a lift, which she accepted. He killed her with a single bullet to the head, the blood sprayed all over the car, and the son of a bitch took her body and threw it on the street. Her son was only two years old when his mother was murdered.

6. A single woman with four children fell madly in love with a much younger man. Shortly after meeting him, she married him and took him into her house with her children. At the start, as always, he was good, but his behavior started to change. He slapped her everywhere they were, in front of whoever was there, and besides this, he began molesting her small daughter. Because of this violation, the girl got pregnant. What I don't understand is why the mother, who knew that her daughter was expecting her own stepfather's child, her grandson, did not report the wretched man. He was sentenced to prison on another charge, and the two of them, the mother and daughter, constantly wrote to him, declaring the love they felt for him.

    After he served his sentence, he got out of prison. His stepdaughter had already given birth to the child, and she had a boyfriend and was back in school, trying to begin a new life for her and the small child. The stepfather went to her house and asked to see the child; thinking nothing was wrong, she and her mother took him to the child's room. Right then he started to check all the messages she had on her phone and found lots of messages from her boyfriend. Without thinking twice, he stabbed her and then cut her throat. He called his brother on the phone to ask for help, saying that he had a problem. The brother hid him in a friend's house, but did not know he had murdered the young girl, the mother of his child. The police came looking for him and explained what was going on. The murderer is in prison once again, for many more years, but his ex-wife lost everything, him, the daughter he killed, her other children and her grandchild, who are now living with another family. I cannot understand why she is still in touch with him in prison. God have mercy on her.

7. As always, when they have just had sex, women like to be spoiled, kissed, and hugged affectionately. One woman, after making love with her husband, wanted him to stay with her in bed a little longer. He wanted to watch sports on television, so he got upset and took a hammer and beat his wife over

seventy times, leaving her body full of holes. This was such a brutal crime that he was sentenced to death. This was one of the most outrageous cases I have seen.

8. To everyone around, they seemed to be a couple who lived very well, according to what his friend said. They arranged to meet at his house, with their wives and children, but the friend waited, and the wife of his friend never appeared. He said that, many years ago, the husband had previously had a record of domestic violence. From the looks of it, the friend was right, because he stabbed his wife and two daughters to death. While the news was on the television showing the paramedics trying to resuscitate one of the daughters, the murderer just stuck a cigarette in his mouth and walked up and down. Everyone, families and friends, was forlorn because they couldn't explain what had happened to him to make him commit this kind of crime.

9. There was a married man who was very violent, and his wife was obliged to separate from him and sought professional help for this. He was in rehabilitation for a few months, and when he got out, he went looking for his wife. When he met her once again, things did not go as he expected; his wife was already with someone else, was very happy, and thought she would start a new life with the other man. He insisted that she take him back, but she said no. Aggressively, he started shaking and pushing her, but at that moment, the boyfriend came in and went to defend her. The ex-husband, without thinking twice, said that if she could not be his, she couldn't be anyone else's; he took out his revolver and shot both of them dead. The solution he found to resolve his problem was to kill them both.

10. Everyone felt very sorry for a man for losing his wife in a very unfortunate way; she hung herself and the poor man found her lifeless body. After some time, this man met another woman, and they were married. She liked to go out and go shopping, because he had money. One day, the husband

called the police from a hotel, asking for help, saying that his wife had disappeared from the hotel where they were sleeping. The police and many volunteers in the area searched for the woman, but found nothing. Then they started to investigate the background and what they found was chilling: this man never got to the hotel with his wife because he left the house alone. He had a girlfriend much younger than his wife, and when she got home from shopping, he hit her on the head with a stone and shot her twice in the head, tied up her body in a sheet, put her in the trunk of the car, took her somewhere far away, and he buried her. By the end of the whole investigation, it was found that he also killed his first wife, all because of the money. He was tried and convicted, and will spend the rest of his life in prison.

Georgia

1. In Atlanta, a man's mother-in-law asked for a court order for protection for her daughter and grandchild, but it did not arrive in time: he killed his wife and small child, and then he killed himself.

2. Also in Atlanta, a couple who had separated were arguing when the man, in a fit of rage, shot the woman dead. He was shot by the police, arrested, and taken to hospital. He is waiting for trial.

Idaho

A man who had just killed his wife was driving along the highway like a lunatic, without knowing where he was going; he hit another car, killing the driver and her four-year-old daughter. After the crash, police found his wife's head in the truck, and her body was found in the garage of the house. He is in prison paying for not just one monstrous crime, but for three murders.

Illinois

1. In Chicago, a woman decided to divorce her husband, who was extremely violent, not only with her but also with the children. He then moved in with his girlfriend. One day the ex-wife told one of her children that she was going to see her ex, and that if she was late coming back, to call the police. When she got to her ex-husband's house, he told his girlfriend to hide in the garage. He and the ex-wife started to argue. He slapped her and started to strangle her until she lost consciousness. He then threw kerosene on her body and set it alight, and with the help of the girlfriend, threw the remains of the body in a river. He was caught by the police.

2. Also in Chicago, a couple were having many problems, as the man drank a lot and beat his wife constantly, accusing her of having sex with other men. Tired of so much abuse and accusations, she decided to leave him. She called the police to tell them she suspected that her husband had pushed his first wife down the stairs, which was how she had died. Furious because she had called the police, he also pushed his second wife down the stairs, killing her. He went to prison.

Indiana

In Indianapolis, a resident called the police to report activities involving drugs and prostitution, but when the authorities arrived there, they found only the bodies of his wife, his mother-in-law, and his four children. He was sentenced to forty years in prison.

Kansas

A woman's family said she was sick with cancer, but there were many problems between her and her husband. She suffered from a lot of physical abuse, according to her sister, but on the other hand, the husband said that his wife was very sick and he no longer knew what to do, because he had lost his job and couldn't pay the hospital bills. He decided to push his wife off from the third floor, and her body fell to the ground, lifeless.

Maryland

1.   A couple lived well and only the husband worked, but as time passed, things began to get difficult and he accumulated a lot of debt. He took out life insurance for his wife, but he was in a hurry to claim the money. For four months, he put car antifreeze in her juice, and little by little, she got more and more sick and died, a sad and painful death. The bastard was given a life sentence.

2.   In Salisbury, a couple owned a company and had an eighteen-year-old daughter. They decided to go out in their boat. When they were out at sea, there was a problem and the boat filled with smoke. Immediately, he took out the lifeboat and helped his wife and daughter to lower it into the water. After they got in it, he said he'd forgotten something and went back onto the boat. He claimed that when he got back, there was no sign of his wife or daughter in the lifeboat. He left in search of help and explained to the authorities what was going on. But they didn't believe him, and when they started to investigate, they discovered that before all this, he had taken out millions of dollars in life insurance for his wife and daughter. The only way to get his hands on this money was to kill them both. The end result is that he is in prison paying for his crime.

Massachusetts

1.   In Boston, a lawyer who was seven months pregnant was leaving a hospital appointment with her husband. They were in a hurry to leave Boston's Brigham and Women's Hospital, as they wanted to get back to their comfortable house in the

suburb of Reading. After two blocks, he stopped the car, and an African American man got in and ordered him to drive to an isolated street. The intruder shot the woman and the man, taking all their jewelry and money. The husband survived, but the wife and baby died. Everyone was very intrigued by this cold blooded murder, killing a pregnant woman. The real story only emerged ten weeks later.

The husband's brother appeared at a police station after being shot and confessed that his brother had made an agreement with two friends of his and had given them a revolver to kill his wife. The brother claimed that he wanted the money from the woman's life insurance to open a restaurant.

2. In bucolic Nantucket Island, a forty-four-year-old woman met an executive. She told her friend about him, saying that he was so handsome, so good, and so intelligent that she felt like she had won the love lottery. But when she heard some comments from another woman who had been with him before and discovered that he was not really a nice person, she called the police to get a protection order so he would not be able to come near her. Two days later, her lifeless body was found in her living room; she had been stabbed many times. The murderer was found a few hours later, drunk driving, and declared he was innocent, but he was arrested.

Michigan

1. A couple had been together all through college, and after they graduated, they decided to marry; everything was wonderful, and they were in love. After their first child was born, things began to cool off, so much so that they separated many times, with him leaving the home and returning after a few days, crying and begging her to let him come back. After one reconciliation, she became pregnant with their second child, and everything seemed to be fine, and there was even a celebration with everyone from both families

gathered together. Whilst everyone was having fun, he took his wife home and shot her in the head, leaving her and the child they were expecting dead. When the police began the investigation, they found divorce documents and also a letter from his lover. They also found out that one day before this party, he had spent the night with the lover. After everything was discovered, he was arrested, tried, convicted, and later sentenced to life imprisonment.

2.   Another couple had known each other since they were very young; they had gone to school together and, after graduating, decided to have a family and were married. As far as society was concerned, they were madly in love, a perfect couple who were doing well financially; he had his own office and she took care of the farm. That was until the day the husband called the police on 911, saying that the family horse had kicked his wife, and she was taken to hospital. As only she knew the truth, she became depressed and the doctor prescribed medication to calm her down. Slowly, she began to get better and everything seemed to be going well. Eighteen months after the accident with the horse, the husband once again called 911, but this time he claimed that his wife had shot herself in the head. Her sister, who had spoken with her before she died, told the police that she had not committed suicide. When they started to investigate, they found a letter from the deceased that claimed that the husband had already tried to kill her several times. The reason was that he had big financial problems, due to giving his lover expensive presents, and the only solution he found was to kill her for her life insurance. He is now paying for his crime.

3.   A husband called the police to report that his wife had been missing for over a month. Authorities and neighbors looked for this woman day and night, and the outcome was very sad: her lifeless body was found, strangled and dismembered. The murderer was her husband, who killed her because she traveled a lot for her job. She left two children, and the murderer is paying for his crime.

Mississippi

A couple in Jacksonville lived well; she worked and had life insurance for $2 million, and he also had a good job at a large company. One day, they went to the beach when a man came up behind them with a gun, demanding all their belongings. The wife tried to disarm the robber, and he shot her in the face and threw her body in the water, and then he shot the husband four times, leaving him unconscious for hours. When he woke up, he pulled his wife's body from the water, took the car, and drove off in search of help. Eventually, he stopped at a store and someone helped him. When the police arrived, the wife was already dead. Her family didn't believe his story and asked the authorities to investigate. It was found that he had debts of almost $60,000 and that he also had a lover. The truth finally came out: they had been arguing because his wife had found out that he had a lover and had asked him for a divorce. After the argument, he asked for forgiveness and then invited her to go to the beach. But when they were on their way, she saw that he had a gun, and it was then that they fought and she was knocked unconscious. He took the revolver and shot her in the face and shot himself four times, all because of the $2 million. Justice was done, and he was sentenced to spend the rest of his life in prison.

Missouri

In Jefferson, a couple had separated and then divorced. He moved into a luxurious apartment close to his ex-wife so he could see his son. The neighbors said that one night they had heard the two arguing. The next day, the husband knocked at the door of his wife's house, and when she opened it, he shot her and killed her. He walked past her body and went up to see his six-year-old son, who was in his room. The father called 911 and gave the phone to his son to speak to the operator. The boy said that his father had killed his mother, and the operator told him to lock himself in the bathroom; after a few seconds, the child told the operator he had heard a shot. His father had killed himself. When the police arrived, they found the two dead bodies, but the boy was fine. This is one of the saddest cases, because at the end of the day, the child had lost his father and his mother, the two most important people in his life.

Nevada

A husband and wife went for a drive and got in an accident; he called 911, crying, weeping, and shouting that his car had fallen in a ravine and his wife was trapped and unable to get out. When help arrived, the woman was already dead. Inconsolable, he was taken to hospital with some injuries, and after being seen to, he went home to rest. The next day, the authorities were investigating and he asked them if they had found his wallet with his documents. The investigation found that what had happened to his wife had not been an accident, but rather murder. He was found guilty.

New Jersey

1. A top executive called 911 to ask for help, saying that his wife had disappeared. Without wasting any time, the police began the search, and not far from where they lived they found her body in her car; she had been physically abused and strangled. The husband was arrested and charged with murder, but he refused to tell the truth, and not even his daughters, who had been in the house, saw what had happened. But he was found guilty and was given thirty years in prison for the brutal murder of his wife.

2. A man apparently lived happily with his wife and their two children, without any problems. Behind But this family had a dark secret that was destroying them. The husband was reported for sexually abusing the two children. Naturally, he should have to pay for his crime, but the court hearing was very painful for the whole family. On the day of the hearing, neither he nor the family appeared. One of their neighbors became curious and went to their house, but when he knocked at the door and no one answered, he pushed open the door

and found the man's dead body; he had a gunshot to the chest, and in the bedroom, the wife and the children were also dead. He had shot his wife and children and then killed himself.

3. Another couple did not seem to have had any problems, but the husband was very jealous, as he was much older than his wife. He called the police, saying that someone had broken into his house, killed his wife, and then tied him up. The police were suspicious; why had they killed the woman but only tied him up? The police soon discovered that the story of the house robbery was untrue and that the real murderer was the husband himself. He had come home from work and found his wife with her bags packed, and when he asked what it meant, she had replied that she could not take all the abuse anymore and was leaving him. At his wits end, thinking that he was going to lose her, he didn't think twice and murdered her. May he pay for his crime.

New York

1. A couple had been living together for a long time. One day, the girlfriend decided to tell him that everything was over. Without saying a word, he left the house; as far as she was concerned, everything was fine. She heard nothing from him for eight days, and then he came back to the house, carrying a bag, kissed her, and came inside. Once inside he opened the bag, stabbed her many times, and walked out of the door with the knife in his hand. As he walked down the street covered in blood, a passer-by saw him and called the police, who arrested him.

2. Another case involved a girl who had always been a good daughter, with the best grades in college, straight A's in all subjects, but she was not so lucky when it came to love.

    After being engaged for a few years, she and her fiancé had broken it off. She met another man, a doctor, who won her heart, and they became engaged. Afterward, he began to change, becoming extremely jealous, manipulative, and very aggressive. When her family saw this, they asked her not to marry him, but when people are in love they never pay any attention and don't care what others say. She decided to get married and moved far away from her family.

Things got worse, the physical abuse began. They never had time to be together. She took a lover, was very happy, and called her family to share her happiness. One day her husband called her family's house, asking after his wife, saying he had arrived home and she wasn't there. This left everyone very worried; her mother, father, brothers, and sisters went in search for her but it was in vain. They went to her house and found her purse with all of her belongings, including her car keys. They reported the husband, but no evidence was found and the case cooled off.

He moved to another state and married someone else, but that didn't last long because he was very violent. He began to go out with another woman, who asked him if he was the one who had killed his wife a few years back, and he was unable to answer; she finished it with him, afraid. As God's justice always arrives, a new judge reopened the case after many years. Her body had never been found, but they managed to prove his guilt and he is now in prison.

3.   A man who had been imprisoned for stabbing his pregnant girlfriend, was freed after completing his sentence. But after he was freed, he began going with another girl, but as time went on, he began to have doubts about her. He thought his girlfriend was betraying him with a lesbian; enraged, took a knife and stabbed her many, many times, not wanting to stop. He confessed the crime to the police, saying that he had cut her body into pieces, put them into a plastic bag, and threw it in the trash.

4. A young girl was in a relationship with her boyfriend and had a child with him. She began to be harassed by a coworker, who started to give her presents and ask her out, but she didn't want to go out with him. In his disappointment, the guy went into a rage, took a knife, raped her, and killed her. Only two months later did he tell where he had left her dead body.

5. A couple was married and later divorced because of their financial problems. He was a millionaire, and a few years later, he met the woman of his dreams and married her. After a few years, they decided to adopt two children. His wife started to become jealous of him with other women and took the children and moved to another country. She fell in love with her electrician and started a romance, telling him about her problems with her husband. After a short while, she divorced her husband, receiving a lot of money in the settlement. The boyfriend asked her to marry him and she accepted, setting the date of the wedding and starting the preparations.

    The day of the ceremony, he told his future wife that he had killed her ex-husband, which made her freeze. The reason was that he was spending her money like crazy and, fearing that it would end, had gone in search of his future wife's ex and had beaten him to death. He told her that he had begged for his life, but the heartless son of a bitch had no pity, leaving him dead, and then he went out with his friends until the next day. The body of the ex was found after three days, when he failed to appear to take the children to school. His driver went to his house, and his car was there he rang the doorbell but no one answered, and when he managed to get in, he found him dead, soaked in blood. For three days no one knew what to make of it, because the ex was a man without enemies. It was a difficult case to resolve as there were no clues, and the authorities let the case get cold.

    The ex-wife, who was now married to this murderer, was not feeling well and went to the doctor; she was diagnosed with cancer, and the doctors tried to cure her, but it was already very advanced. After she died, the husband was arrested and started to talk about how he had killed his wife's ex. The police reopened the case, and this time he was given a life sentence.

6. A single woman who had a child met a man who was not to her parents' liking, but she liked him and started going out with him. At the time her son was just two years old. As always everything started well, but then the physical abuse began, and her only small son saw it many times. Over time, they moved away and things became more serious between them, and they had three more children. They were more or less well off, even having a small business together, but the abuse never stopped, because he drank and took drugs. Money was always the problem, and one day they received some money for doing a job. He arrived home drunk and started shouting, asking her for the money, but she said she didn't know about it, and so a fight began. Seeing this, her son tried to defend his mother. The stepfather pushed him away and the boy fell, but as he continued to beat his mother, the boy got up and called the police. He was no longer a two-year-old child, unable to do anything to defend his mother. He was sixteen years old. As the police didn't come, his stepfather continued beating his mother. The boy ran up to his room to find something to defend his mother and grabbed a pair of scissors; he went downstairs and cut his stepfather on the arm. They began to fight, but when the police arrived, they found the man stabbed to death. It was the sixteen-year-old boy who killed him. This mother lost the man she had lived with for fourteen years, and father to three of her children, and lost her eldest son, who was imprisoned for many years for the murder of his stepfather.

7. A couple lived very well for thirty years of their married life. He owned some businesses, and their neighbors said they lived happily and always went on vacation to their summer house. Problems began, and he started to beat her, threatening to kill her with a knife. She was suffering so much that she told her neighbor because she was afraid. The neighbor advised her

to leave her husband, and she decided to divorce him. When she told her husband she wanted a divorce, he took a knife and stabbed her many times, leaving her dead. Then he tried to kill himself with the same knife, but he recovered in the hospital and had to pay for his crime.

8. A man was living with his girlfriend, who had a young son and was eight months pregnant. They got in an argument and he strangled her. He said that he took a belt, put it round her throat, and tightened it until she fell down dead. Then he told her six-year-old child to fill the bathtub with water, saying he was going to teach him how to swim; he held the child's head under the water until he stopped breathing. Then he tried to commit suicide by opening the gas oven, but as he didn't die; he is now in prison to pay for the three crimes he committed.

9. A mother was celebrating the birthday of one of her children, who was then fifteen years old. It was a special day, and that was why her husband was father was there. But he was not supposed to be there, because although they were married and had six children, domestic violence was always present; they fought a lot and the police were always called to calm things down. On the day of the birthday party, he decided to attack his wife with an axe, in front of everybody. The children were afraid that their mother was dying, but she recovered. The father is still on the run from the law.

10. A woman was left by her husband with two children, a girl of fourteen and a boy of eight. She met a new man and started dating him. One day her boyfriend took advantage of the fact that the girl was alone and tried to force himself on her. At that moment the mother and brother arrived, and he started to strangle his girlfriend, leaving her unconscious, and cut the eight-year-old boy's head off with an axe. The daughter called the police, and when they arrived, they knocked down the door and found a bloodbath. The murderer was sleeping on the couch in the nude; they found the dead body of his

girlfriend, and in a plastic bag was the mutilated and headless body of the boy. The injured girl was taken to hospital, where she recovered, but now she must live without her mother or brother.

11. A couple decided to get a divorce. In an argument over child support money for the children, the ex-husband became enraged, punched the woman many times, and shot her three times in the head, killing her. He also attacked a friend of the family who witnessed the crime, who ended up in hospital. But the man was not satisfied and appeared at the hospital, telling the victim that if he lodged a complaint with the police, he would also kill him, his wife, and child. As this man was a policeman with the New York Police Department, he thought things would be different for him, but he is in prison, paying for his crime.

12. An eighteen-year-old girl had a crush on a tall, and good-looking boy, who was nineteen years old. They met in a bar, and after two hours talking together, they left hand in hand. The body of the young girl was found in Central Park, and on the other side of the street, the boy was found with his chest, stomach, and face all scratched. When he was interrogated by the police, he said he had been scratched by a cat and that the marks on his hand were caused by a floor cleaning machine. After seven hours of interrogation, he confessed that he had accidentally killed the girl. The police discovered that he took drugs and was a thief, but appearances are always deceptive. He has now been released, after serving five years in prison.

13. A very respected policeman was married with two children, one of them already grown up. Things between the husband and wife were not going very well, but they were trying to keep the family together. Some men need to have another woman elsewhere, and this is what happened. Far from his home, he met a young girl who lived with her parents, her two sisters, and her small child; she was a single mother and

had been let down during her youth, but she was working and everything was well with her family, who were very poor but very close. There was a lot of affection, unity, respect, and love in this house, until she met this policeman and her life changed forever. They met in the restaurant where she worked. They started going out together, and he met her son and her parents, who didn't agree with this relationship, because he was a married man and much older. He was very manipulative and domineering; he beat her, leaving marks over all of her body, and she became terrified of him. Afraid that her parents would find out about the violence she was suffering, she broke it off with him. Then she found another boyfriend. The policeman went crazy with jealousy and was more violent than ever. One day, as she was walking to work, her ex drove up in his car, stopped, and ordered her to get in. She was afraid of him, so she got in the car, finding a bunch of flowers on the seat. She asked him who those flowers were for, but he didn't answer and continued driving the car; she asked where he was taking her, as she was late for work. He continued without any kind of response, and she realized that her life was in danger. She started to cry and asked him to go back. He stopped the car, took his revolver, and shot her in the head. The blood sprayed all over the inside of the car; he opened the passenger door and dumped her body in the park.

As if nothing had happened, he went back home, changed clothes, and went to work. While he was at work, the girl's mother called the police station looking for her, and when he answered the phone, she asked where her daughter was as she never went work that day. He said that he didn't know where she was.

The next day, two federal agents turned up at his house and arrested him, but not for long. He was released on bail of $50,000. After a few months, his wife was called to testify and everyone was surprised when she tried to put the blame on her own son in an attempt to save her husband, the murderer.

But all their plans went up in smoke when the son was called to testify, and the prosecuting attorney pressed him. The judge declared the policeman guilty and he was given a life sentence.

14. A couple had been living a long time with violence, she had her mouth all smashed up, eyes, face, and body marked; there was such violence that she feared for her own life. They had two children, one was five years old from her first relationship, and the second, a girl who was only a few months old, that she had had with this new boyfriend. Not knowing what to do, she ran to her brother's house, told him what was happening with her boyfriend and that she knew that death was near. She was brutally murdered by her boyfriend some time later. Justice was also done in this case, and he is in prison.

15. After separating from his wife, a husband was forced to pay for the upkeep of the children, and in desperation, he went to see his wife. Without thinking too much, he shot her several times when she was going out to work, leaving her dead. Then he went to look for the people who were involved in the child support case and killed both of the women. Lastly, he shot himself and died, leaving the children without their father or mother.

16. After separating because of the abuse of her husband, a woman became a single mother; she was very proud of this and began to forget the bad times she had gone through with her ex. When she least expected it, a new Prince Charming appeared, and she thought she should give him a chance and decided to get married. Another child was born of this happy union; her first child was thirteen years old, and everything was just fine with the four in the family. But the happiness didn't last long, and the problems began again. She tried to leave him, to take care of her children just like the first time. But this man wouldn't accept the separation and became enraged; he took a hammer and killed her along with her thirteen-year-old son.

17. In another murder case, a couple had two girls, one who was five years old and the other who was three. On the day of the tragedy, they went out to celebrate their daughter finishing the school year. He stopped the car to take photos, leaving the engine running in a very deserted and dangerous place, with a steep drop. He later said that his wife wanted to kill herself; if he knew this, why not seek professional help? Leaving the car engine running with her and the two daughters inside by a steep drop confirmed that this man was a dangerous person. If one of their daughters tried to kill herself, would he also plan how to do it? I have no doubt that this man should pay for the crime he committed.

18. In the basement of a woman's house lived her sister, her husband, and their child. Her brother-in-law was a very jealous, manipulative, authoritarian, and aggressive man, and the sister was afraid of him. They were always fighting, but she did not take the trouble to find out why they were fighting. One morning, when she went to see her sister, she found her dead body; the brother-in-law had disappeared. At her wits end, she asked for help and she believes that her brother-in-law is in hiding at his parents' house.

19. A couple with two children came to the United States in search of the American dream, but behind that pleasant looking couple there was a dark side that only they knew about: domestic violence. It got to the point where the woman couldn't take any more and decided to leave her husband. She moved into a small apartment with her daughter. One day, her husband arrived and took out a gun and shot her in the head; she instantly fell down dead. Berserk, he went to his car, loaded the revolver once more, returned to the apartment, and shot himself in the head; he fell to the ground next to the body of his dead wife. This all took place in front of their daughter.

20. A twelve-year-old girl became involved with a man of twenty, with a record of drugs and robbery. He was in and out of

prison, and whenever he returned from prison, she received him with open arms, and he always left marks all over her body. One day he stabbed her in the back, cut her neck and wrist, and threw himself from the fifth floor stairs, but he survived. He is now paying for his crime.

21. All the women of the world should take more care with the partners they choose to bring into their homes. To tell the truth, we don't really know ourselves, and since we often do things that surprise us, how can we trust people we have just met? One woman knew a man for less than a year and brought him to live in her apartment. To everyone else, they did not seem to have a problem, and no one ever heard of any kind of violence, until one night the neighbor heard a shot and called the police. When they arrived, the police found her dead, with one shot to the head by her boyfriend. Her friends thought she was the best person in the world. Her murderer was arrested there in the apartment.

22. A couple left their country in 1999 in search of the American dream, along with their daughter. They separated some time later, and she stayed with the children and managed to get work as a cleaner so she could take care of them. Tired of being alone and needing the help of another, she put an ad in a newspaper, hoping to meet someone who suited her. She quickly found the man she thought would be her Prince Charming, who said he was a doctor. Whilst they were dating, he convinced his beloved to take out three life insurance policies, each one for a million dollars, and if anything happened to her, he would be the sole beneficiary. I cannot believe there are so many stupid women these days. Her dead body was found in her room, and the man collected millions of dollars and took off to his country of origin. According to the autopsy, she died from a heart problem but the diagnosis of the cause of death was later changed to "unknown."

23. A girl was just sixteen years old when she started going out with a much older policeman; he knew the law and knew that

what he was doing was not right. The girl's mother was always against it because she knew he abused her and was always threatening her. A few days after her daughter broke off with him and got another boyfriend, the ex took the young girl's life and then killed himself.

24. In Oklahoma, a husband claimed that then he got home from work, he found his wife unconscious. Beside himself, he picked up the phone and called the emergency services. While he waited for help, he tried to give her mouth to mouth resuscitation, but it was no use because when the ambulance arrived, she was pronounced dead. The husband cried like a madman, saying a thief had come into the house to steal things and had killed his wife. All the neighbors felt sorry for him and were worried by the fact that a neighbor had been murdered by an intruder, putting an end to their peace of mind. But the investigation revealed that the real culprit was the husband himself, who is now in prison, paying for his crime.

25. In Middletown, Orange County, there was a single mother with four children to raise. She worked seven days a week to feed her children. Her ex, enraged that she had finished with him, contracted a man to kill her. On Christmas Eve a man mercilessly shot her many times. The case was investigated and resolved, with both the murderer and the man who contracted him being imprisoned for their crime.

26. In Putnam Valley, a couple had a fourteen-year-old daughter, and everything seemed to be just fine; the husband worked at a good company, and his wife tried to help out, selling her artwork over the Internet.

When he was laid off from his job, they began to have problems, and when he developed health problems requiring medication, the conflict got worse. He didn't know how to sort things out and thought that the only solution was to kill his wife and their daughter and then take his own life.

27. In Yonkers, a couple had separated and was going through the divorce process. The ex-husband moved to Atlanta, and one day he hired a taxi to drive him from Georgia to see his ex-wife. When she heard the doorbell ring and looked through the window, she was alarmed to see her ex-husband. Not knowing what to do and without thinking properly in that moment, she opened the door and he came in, and they sat in the dining room to talk. All of a sudden, he took out a gun and shot his wife eleven times, and then he shot himself in the head. When the police arrived, they found the two dead bodies.

Ohio

1. A woman asked for a divorce from her husband because she could no longer bear the problems they were having. A few months earlier, the police had been to their house because of domestic violence. After the separation, the husband began to act strangely, according to the neighbors, and it seemed that he could not stand his wife not being there. He went to the school where she taught, and in front of all the pupils, he stabbed and shot her many times leaving her almost dead. Afterward, he went home, and when the police arrived hours later, they found him with a shot to the head in the garage. His wife's lawyer said that days before, his client was terrified and afraid that something like this would happen. He was hospitalized in critical condition.

2. A man had been arrested and was being interrogated at the station. He said that he went to his girlfriend's house, that they had begun to fight, and that she pushed him twice. He admitted pushing her back, and she fell. He said he called several times for an ambulance, but when there was no reaction, he tried to give her CPR, but without success. They asked him why he had not called the police, and he answered that his phone was broken and that the battery of his girlfriend's phone had no charge, and not knowing what

to do, he took her and wrapped her in a blanket, put her in his car, and only came home the next morning. They asked him what had become of his son who was only two and a half years old, and he answered that he had left him in the house, alone. They also asked him what he had done with his girlfriend, who was expecting. The case was only closed after his two-and-a-half-year-old son told his grandmother that he had seen his mother's body wrapped in a sheet. He was convicted on the basis of this declaration.

3. A couple had two children; she was a housewife and he was a respected policeman. Everything between them seemed to be going well until one day the husband called 911, saying that his wife had disappeared. For the family and friends who knew her, it was hard to believe, her disappearance was impossible, because she was very strict with their children and would not have left her children alone in the house for anything in the world. Everyone suspected the husband, and they asked for professional help. Investigators found her dead body and discovered that he had murdered her in her own house, in their own bed, while she was sleeping. They found the poor thing in her pajamas. The husband is paying for his crime.

4. In Kent, a young boy who was riding in the car with his mother and small brother. Unfortunately, there was an accident, and his mother and brother died instantly, but the boy was thrown out of the back window; he did not die, although his face was badly deformed, and he spent a long time in hospital. When he got out, he inherited $3 million, but this was no comfort to him because everyone called him "Scarface," and the so-called "friends" around him were only interested in his money. Even his girlfriend hired some friends to lie to him, telling him that she was pregnant and that she wanted money to have an abortion. Without thinking very much, he gave her the money as he thought they were too young to have children. A few weeks later, he came home and they started to argue, and in her anger she told him she had never liked him, that

the pregnancy was all a lie, that she had arranged it with her friends to get his money. Enraged and unable to believe what he was hearing, he asked her to return all of the money, but she replied that she had spent it. Horrified, he took out his revolver and shot her in the face. A few hours later, he called her mother to say that her daughter had committed suicide, but her mother did not believe her daughter had done this. At the beginning of the investigation, he denied he had killed her, but later he confessed the whole story and was sentenced to twenty years in prison.

Oregon

They were a model couple, working together to get on in life, and they were very happy. One day the neighbors were alarmed to see that their house was catching fire and called the fire department. It took twenty minutes for them to get there, and when they arrived, everything had burnt down. The wife's body was found in the ashes, but the husband was not found. He turned up afterward, saying that he had woken up early and gone to the store to buy some things for the house, leaving his wife resting. In his defense, he brought the receipt to prove that he was telling the truth. The neighbors told the authorities that the day before they had heard the couple arguing. Another problem was that the firm where the husband worked was going to be transferred to another country and he wanted to start a new life, but the wife wanted to stay behind. His solution was to open all the gas taps in the house, causing the explosion and the death of his wife. He is paying for the crime he committed.

Pennsylvania

1. A man and woman were living together, and one day he wanted his girlfriend to cook for him, but she did not want to. He became upset and threw the microwave oven at her, beat her, and tried to strangle her. She was taken to hospital, where she died from the blows.

2. Another couple had been married for many years and had three children, who were already grown up. They were a close family and very religious; the wife went to church every Sunday. But things began to change between the husband and wife, and one day, the husband came home with an envelope that had been left in his car, with a letter from a man claiming he was having an affair with his wife. The woman vigorously denied everything, and the children were surprised at what they heard; they trusted their mother completely and believed that what they were hearing was impossible. But the envelopes continued arriving, with photos and letters, and the husband was getting more and more aggressive, until one day everyone had gone out and only the two of them were in the house. She discovered that it was her own husband that had been sending the letters, torturing her with these false accusations. Realizing he was in danger because she was going to report him, the only solution he found was to kill his wife. He took the dog's lead and strangled her; he put her body in the car and drove it away, leaving it abandoned in the car. Everything was discovered, and he received a life sentence. Their children were devastated that their own father was their mother's killer.

3. A man who worked for the government was having an affair with a secretary. One day he invited her out to dinner and then to the house where he lived, and it was there that the awful thing happened. He said that another woman came into the house with a revolver in her hand, and that they began to fight each other and the revolver accidentally went off, killing his lover. This was all made up, because he tried to get rid of her body. Proof was found that this man had murdered his lover out of jealousy, and she had said he was a maniac and that she was going to leave him; when he heard this, his solution was to kill her.

Texas

1. A woman owned a small bakery, had a seven-year-old son, and was also seven months pregnant with the child of her ex-boyfriend, who was already married. Her family and friends planned the baby shower. On the day, everyone waited for hours, but she never appeared. The police started a search and found blood in her house but no sign of anyone having forced the door to enter the residence. The police interrogated her ex-boyfriend, who was very nervous, and he confessed he had killed them, took her car, put the bodies in, and left them thrown there, just because she wanted him to divorce his wife.

2. A couple lived very well; the man had married a woman of higher social status than he. Their first daughter was born and the whole family was very happy, and then a second one came along, but then things started to change, as he had met a much younger woman. He left his wife and went to live with his new lover, giving her a very expensive ring. From what he himself said, he went back and forth between the two women, until one day he told his lover that he was trying to make it work with his wife, for the well-being of the children. She accepted this, but I think his decision was planned because, when he returned to his house, the wife started to become ill and was in a lot of pain. One night, when his wife started to cry in pain, he took her to hospital, seeming to be very worried. Another day, he woke up to find his wife being sick and crying, and again he took her to hospital. At the hospital, the father, mother, brother, and sister-in-law were very worried. Then they talked to the doctor, who had discovered that the food she had been eating was poisoned. They were dumbstruck and asked themselves who would want to kill her, but her brother was very suspicious of the brother-in-law. He went to his sister's house and emptied the fridge, taking all the food to the laboratory, but no type of poison was found. They hoped she would get better, but she died a few days later. Incensed, her family hired a lawyer, as they knew the

husband had something to do with her death. He discovered that he had bought snake poison, and little by little he had poisoned the woman. He was sentenced to life in prison.

3. A nurse decided to divorce her husband, but they had two children, and her husband was fighting for their custody. The children lived with the mother, and the father had them on weekends; everything seemed to be going very well. But one day, she was supposed to pick up the children from her ex-husband's house after work; he waited but she didn't show up; he was worried because she was normally punctual. He decided to go to her house to find out what was going on, but she wasn't there either. The husband was questioned by the police and said that he was with the children the whole time. The police investigated many other people, as many people had been implicated in the case. Then one day, one of the children said that they thought their father had killed their mother, because on the day of the crime he took them to have dinner at a friend's house, returning much later, and that later on that day, he woke up in the middle of the night and went to look for his father but he wasn't in the house either. With the help of the children, the case was investigated, and he is now paying for his crime.

4. This crime took twenty-five years to be resolved. A man was married and had two children. One day, their son knocked on the door of his parents' room with his school grades, which had to be signed by one of them; the father took the paper and signed it, but the mother was facing away from the door and didn't move. He left the room, took his books, and went to catch the bus, but as soon as he left, the father dragged his wife's body out of the house, put her in the trunk of the car, and left as if for work, driving past the school bus-stop, waving to the children. In the afternoon, after work, he threw his wife's body in a deserted place and returned home as if nothing had happened. Two days later, the body of a man who had been accused of being with his wife was also found dead. There were a lot of investigations, but they were unable

to prove who the murderer was. After twenty-five years, it was discovered that the real murderer was the husband himself, because his wife had found him having sex with their adopted daughter and had indignantly threatened to report him. Thank goodness, justice was done and he is in prison, paying for his crime.

Utah

In Salt Lake City, a man who was addicted to drugs killed his pregnant wife, shooting her in the head, after she found out that he had not been accepted to medical school, as he claimed. When her body was found three months later, there was very little left of it. His mother-in-law asked him how he had been able to do something like that to her daughter, and he said that she was the best thing that had happened in his life, and he didn't know why he had committed the crime, not only against his wife, but also against the unborn child.

Virginia

A night of despair began for one woman back when she met a man and started going out with him. It was not long before they were married. It was then that he became possessive and extremely violent; things became much worse when he physically and mentally started to abuse their child. She decided to divorce him, and her life became hell. He watched her twenty-four hours a day, wherever she went, and became worse still when he learned that she was going out with someone else. He became like a demon, threatening not only her but also their fifteen-year-old son. She decided to send their son to a military academy, hoping that nothing would happen to him there. But she was not so lucky; he told his friends that one day he would kill her. One Friday, she was in her beauty salon where she worked with her fiancé, and the ex killed her right there with several shots, put the fiancé in hospital with severe wounds, and then, with a single bullet, took his own life.

Washington

There was a couple who was very comfortable financially and lived a seemingly happy life with their two daughters. But the wife suffered a lot because her husband was violent and manipulative, and everything had to be done the way he wanted it. Unable to take so much abuse, she decided to divorce him; after a few years, she rebuilt her life with another man. Together, they bought a house in Washington and moved in with her two daughters. After a few months, she became pregnant with quadruplets. When these children were born, everybody was very happy. One day, when one of their daughters got home from school, she opened the door and went in, calling for her mother. There was no answer, so she started looking for her throughout the house. She found her mother's body all covered in blood on the floor, and she immediately called the police and said that her mother was dead. At first, the new husband was a suspect, but after interrogating him for five hours, they found he had nothing to do with his wife's death. Then they started to investigate the ex-husband, and the truth started to come out. The ex had lied to one of his employees, telling him that his wife treated the daughters badly and that he wanted to be recognized as their father, and the only way for this to happen was if his ex were to die. Even for the price of $14,000, the employee could not find the courage to commit the crime and had paid a few thousand dollars to his cousin for him to do it. The cousin drove around for hours and hours with the address given by the ex, asking here and there until he found the house, went up and, without any pity, went in and found the poor woman going out with a basket of laundry to wash. She took one shot to the jaw, and even then she had still tried to run and save her life, but it was in vain, because he managed to catch her and finished the job he had been paid to do, cutting her throat. As God's justice never fails, all those involved paid for their crime with a life sentences.

Other Countries

Australia

This case took place in Newtown, a suburb of Sydney. According to the husband, his wife and two friends arrived at the airport, put their suitcases in the car, and drove to their country house. They left their belongings in the room and went out, when there was a rainstorm. After a few days, blood was found on the room carpet, but the husband said that some kerosene from a portable heater had spilled on it, and instead of cleaning it, he had decided to throw out the carpet. One of his wife's friends called him and asked him if he knew where her daughter was, because she hadn't shown up. The husband answered that she had gone to Denmark with her mother, which surprised her, as she was her mother and knew nothing of this. But there was another friend that his wife trusted with her secrets, whom she had said, if something like this happened some day it would not have been an accident, because her husband was cheating on her, and she had already hired a detective, who had taken photos of her husband kissing a lover. Even with all this, the police ignored the case as they had not found sufficient proof. Everything came to light when a worker who was cleaning snow from the highway in the storm saw fragments of bones in a clearing in a very remote place. He called the police and took them to the place, and they found an envelope with the name of his wife, fresh bones, and also two of the victim's teeth. The husband was sentenced to fifty years in prison.

Brazil

1. A woman who was a journalist had been secretly dating a work colleague for two years. When her father found out that this was going on, he was upset because the colleague was sixty years old, but as his daughter was an independent person, he ended up accepting their relationship. After four years, she ended this relationship, but the man was unable to accept this. Upset, he went to her house and beat her savagely; her father called the police, who made a record stating that she

had been assaulted. A few days later, he turned up again at her home to ask her forgiveness for everything he had done. And as the daughter did not want any more problems, the father treated him as well as he could. He said good-bye and left, but a few days later he returned, and in a very friendly way, they invited him to have lunch. They sat at the table, the daughter served him, and the father took the opportunity to ask him to leave his daughter alone, but this was the last time he saw his daughter alive. She was murdered with a shot to the back and another in her ear, without any chance to defend herself. Those who die lose their lives, but the father lost his precious treasure and the murderer is free and waiting on an appeal.

2. A couple had been together for almost two years, and her sister was very concerned by his controlling behavior: he was terribly jealous of his girlfriend, always saying things about the clothes she wore, not wanting her to talk to any other man, so much so that they split up. Their relationship ended and restarted several times; even when they were separated, he followed her everywhere. He said he loved her and was afraid of losing her. One day she decided to tell him she was going out with another man, but he shot her, and with the same gun, shot himself in the head, dying the next day in hospital.

3. When a man's girlfriend became pregnant, things changed; he did not want to marry her or live with her. He accepted the child that was to be born, but not the daughter she had from another relationship. After the baby was born, he got custody and took the child away. She went to court and got a court order from the judge with permission to see the child. When he received the summons, he went crazy and shot her once, killing her. He disappeared with her body for four days. He is now in prison, serving a fifteen-year sentence.

4. There was a woman who was dynamic, hardworking, and very happy, and her husband was too, until the day he lost his job. He started to drink and became an alcoholic. His wife had a small store and earned enough money to pay all their

bills. But by now the husband no longer wanted to work, and the wife became tired of this situation. After nine years of marriage, she was forced to ask for a separation, but this decision cost her life. One month after the divorce, she was found dead in her own bed with a shot to her face. After he had committed the crime, he called his brother-in-law and confessed that he had killed his wife. But the worst of it is that he is on the run from justice, but she lost her life.

5.   A married man's family life began to fall apart because he started drinking. His children left the house because their father was very aggressive, and the mother also could not take the abuse and asked for a separation. He did not want to accept this, but she left their home, and he always called with the excuse that he wanted to talk to the children. After six months of being separated, he convinced his wife to celebrate their youngest daughter's birthday, who would be four years old. The party was held at his friend's house; he bought a cake, made a barbecue, and they spent the whole day having fun. But all of a sudden, he began to stab his wife with a knife and killed her, then fled and disappeared for months. Her daughter cannot accept the situation and is seeking justice so that he pays for the death of her mother.

Egypt

A couple took a vacation that ended in tragedy. At the hotel where they were staying, the girlfriend was discovered on the bed, unable to breathe, and the doctors could not diagnose what was wrong. She died, and a few months later, he returned home to the house where they had lived together, but her car was missing. The police found the car not far from where he lived, and when they examined it, they found a bag containing enough cyanide to kill five hundred people. Before he was tried, it was discovered that he had killed two other two women, and he was the beneficiary of a $6 million insurance policy. He was convicted and given a life sentence.

Spain

1. In Madrid, a couple separated because the boyfriend had physically abused his partner for a long time. But as he did not want to lose her, he went to a television station and asked for her hand in marriage, which she did not accept. Once again he reacted with violence. Four days later her body was found in the elevator of her building, with her throat slit. He was convicted and will pay for his crime.

2. A husband who was a little older than his wife ran a small business with her. Everything was going well until the day when he discovered that his wife was having an affair with another man, but they stayed together. With time, their business began to go downhill, and they were obliged to close it. Instead of being in charge, they were now employees, and they both went out to work every day; things seemed to be better between them. One day, his wife was late in coming home, and her husband tried to call her on the phone, but she did not answer, and this left him very angry, because of what had happened in the past. When she got home some hours later, they began to argue, and without answering back, she went to the bedroom and began packing her bags. When he realized she was really leaving him, he went crazy and said he would rather see her dead. He took a piece of wood and started beating her and did not stop. When he saw that she was dead, he took her body and her suitcases and put them in the car, and then he drove for many hours in order to dispose of her body. When he returned home, he cleaned up all the evidence and then called emergency services, saying that his wife had disappeared and that he needed their help to find her. When the police began to interrogate him, the authorities suspected that he had killed his wife because of jealousy. He couldn't deny it, confessed to having killed her, and was sentenced to life imprisonment.

Guatemala

After being married for twenty-five years, a husband was forbidden from entering his house because of the domestic violence he had inflicted on his family. But the husband entered the house secretly, took a knife, and brutally murdered his wife and their daughters, aged nineteen and twelve. Unconcerned, he turned himself in and said he was ready to pay for his crimes.

Honduras

1. A couple who had lived together for many years had three children, but things between them were not going very well because the husband was violent. When she could take no more of his beatings, she decided to leave him and try to start a new life for her and her children. After a party, he came home drunk and asked her to come back to him, but when she said no, he became enraged, killed her and her brother, and then killed himself.

2. Another man suspected that his wife was being unfaithful, and so he killed her as well as his mother-in-law and then killed himself. These men nowadays have to stop assuming things about their wives. There has to be trust in a relationship, and they should not let jealousy and mistrust make them commit a crime.

3. A couple had been married for a long time, but because of the husband's heavy drinking and physical abuse, his wife decided to separate from him. Unfortunately this was not enough to stop the abuse, as he went to her new house to insult her. One day he drank more than he should have and turned up at her house with a gun. Desperate and very afraid, she tried to take the gun from his hand, but he pulled the trigger and killed her. When the police arrived, the man was covered in blood on the floor, crying in regret, but it was all too late. He is now in prison, paying for his crime.

Mexico

1.   A husband said that he had been driving to cross the US border and a group of men had beaten him so much that when he woke up and looked for his wife, he couldn't find her anywhere. He asked for help from the police. In making his statement, something didn't seem right, because when the police asked to see the marks on his body, there weren't any. They decided to accompany him back to Mexico and found blood everywhere in his residence. There was evidence that he had killed his wife in the house and then threw her body in the river, and he ended up confessing to this. He was convicted and will pay for his crime. He never revealed why he murdered her.

2.   A man who wrote horror novels lived in the capital. The police went to his apartment because his girlfriend had disappeared, and when they arrived they found her thorax in the closet, her legs in the fridge, and some bones in a cereal box. The title of his latest novel was *Cannibal Instinct*. The man told the police that he had cooked and eaten some parts of his girlfriend's body and that the other parts were spread around the apartment. He is also being investigated for another three cases of mutilation. The police said that he had tried to escape when they went into the apartment, but that he had been run over by a car, suffering minor injuries, and that he confessed his crimes. He was convicted and will pay for the murders.

3.   An American couple and their three children spent their vacation in Mexico, and everyone was very happy, going to all kinds of places to see the beauty of Mexico. One day, one of the girls wanted to go out, but her mother was not feeling well, and so the father took the three daughters and went out with them. After they got in the car, the father said that he had forgotten something and went back to the hotel for a few minutes. Tired of waiting for her father, the daughter decided to go and see what he was doing, and when she tried to open the door, it was locked from the inside. She knocked on the

door, and her father opened it and told her to go wait for him in the car. She saw that he had changed his shirt, and after a few minutes, he came back to the car and they went on a beautiful trip to Mexico City, and they had a lot of fun. When they returned to the hotel, the father made a point that the girls should go into the room first, where they found the body of their mother laid out, with hammer blows to the head and all over her body. She had been killed by their own father a few hours earlier. He denied it, saying that he had nothing to do with the murder of his wife, that the murderer had been his lover many years before, who was not a woman but rather a man. Both of them are paying for their crime.

Peru

1. A man lived with his wife and their child, but they were always fighting. One day they started to argue, and the enraged husband took an axe and started hacking at his wife all over her body, all of this in front of their ten-year-old son, who ran out of the house, yelling that his father was killing his mother. When everyone arrived, she was already dead, with her head severed from her body, and he had disappeared.

2. A married man who was very violent returned home drunk one day and started to beat his wife and their children. Trying to defend herself, she took a knife and stabbed him repeatedly. She was imprisoned for the crime she committed, even though it was in self-defense.

3. In spite of the best treatment that their wives give them at home, men always look for similar treatment elsewhere. One man managed to find a new woman and made her his lover for a long time, and they even had a child together, but things deteriorated when she began to pressure him to recognize his paternity of the child, and this was one thing he did not want. He killed her and buried her in the yard of the house where he lived with his wife. When she was cleaning the yard, the

dog began to dig and found the body of the husband's lover buried there. Worst of all, the child had disappeared, and the authorities think it is possible he also killed his own son.

Puerto Rico

1. A husband loved his wife so much that he was even jealous of her shadow. One night, when he got home from work and she wasn't in the house, he waited. When she got home, without asking any questions, he shot her in the head five times and then killed himself.

2. A couple went on vacation to Puerto Rico. The jealous husband killed his wife and their daughter by beating them. The guy had the nerve to say that he had wanted to kill everyone but didn't have the time. He said he wanted to kill the other children, of two, three, and five years, but the police arrived and stopped him.

Domestic Violence in the Maria da Penha Law. Reflections on the Visibility of the Judiciary in Family Conflicts Between the Sexes in Brazil

The trivialization of domestic violence, its conception as an inexorable part of relations between couples (which includes any kind of intimate partnership), and even of relationships involving noncouples, considering the construction of gender that makes women objects, denying them as being subject to the law and the autonomy of someone able to make their own choices, including that of putting an end to a relationship, are factors that impede the recognition of gender violence, making it invisible not only for the victims, who accept their "biological destiny," but also to society and to the State, to the extent that they deny the existence of a social and public health problem, needs institutional action to raise awareness on prevention and eradication. Everything would indicate that the saying still prevails to "not become involved in fights between husband and wife."

The visibility of gender violence in a domestic setting demands the recognition of violence against women as a violation of human rights, a violation that involves serious damage to the physical and mental health of the victims and, as such, requires coordinated inter-disciplinary intervention, as much as any other social problem faced at an institutional level. In other words, conflict of gender must be de-privatized, highlighting the relationship of power imposed by the violence in a domestic setting and making it palpable.

And it is precisely this that the recent Law no. 11.340/06, also known as the "Maria da Penha Law," tries to do, seeking to offer assistance to women who are victims of domestic violence, including not only measures of a criminal and criminal procedure nature, but also protective measures for the victim and their family members along with any witnesses (articles 18 to 24). Complementing the network of public policies necessary to face the problem, it also includes measures for the prevention and the raising of awareness in a general way—educational campaigns—as well as specific measures aimed at raising awareness among individuals working within the legal, academic and law enforcement sectors (article 8), as well as assistance to victims of violence (article 9).

Silva, Danielle Martins. "Domestic Violence in the Maria da Penha Law. Reflections on the Visibility of the Judiciary in Family Conflicts Between the Sexes." *Jus Navigandi, Teresina*, 12, 1874, August 18, 2008. Available at <http://jus2.uol.com.br/doutrina/texto.asp?id=11614>. Accessed on January 28, 2010.

In Brazil, in the definition of the Belém do Para Convention (Inter-American Convention to Prevent, Punish and Eradicate Violence Against Women, adopted OAS in 1994), violence against women is an "act or conduct, based on gender, which causes death or physical, sexual or psychological harm or suffering to women, whether in the public or the private sphere." Violence against women is a manifestation of the historically unequal power relations between women and men that lead to the domination and discrimination against women by men and which impede the full progress of women."

The United Nations Conference on Human Rights (Vienna, 1993) formally recognized violence against women as a violation of human rights. Since then, the governments of the member countries of the UN and nonprofit organizations have worked for the elimination of this kind of violence, which is also recognized as a serious public health problem. According to the World Health Organization, "the consequences of abuse are deep, going beyond the health and happiness of the individual and are affecting the well-being of entire communities."

Brazilian Criminal Code

The Brazilian Criminal Code says that sexual violence can be characterized either physically, psychologically, or as a threat, and includes rape, attempted rape, seduction, violence, and acts of obscenity. The stages of domestic violence constitute a cycle which can become a vicious circle, repeating itself over months or years. Firstly there is the stage of tension, which accumulates and is manifested through tension, full of insults and threats, which are often reciprocal. Then comes the stage of aggression, as an uncontrolled discharge of all that accumulated tension. The aggressor attacks the victim with pushes, punches, and kicks, or sometimes uses objects such as a bottle, stick, iron bar, or others. Then comes the stage of reconciliation, in which the aggressor asks for forgiveness and promises to change their behavior, or pretends that nothing happened, but is more affectionate and kind, gives presents, and makes the woman believe that it won't happen again. And frequently this cycle is repeated, each time with greater violence and at shorter intervals between the stages. Experience shows that this cycle can be repeated indefinitely; worst of all, it often ends in tragedy, with serious injury or even the murder of the woman.

Texts transcribed from http://copodeleite.rits.org.br/apc-aa-patricia galvao/home/mapadosite.shtml. Accessed December 2009.

Men and Violence against Women

Violence is often considered a typically male manifestation, a kind of "instrument for the resolution of conflicts."

The roles taught since childhood mean that boys and girls learn to deal with emotions differently. Boys are taught to repress manifestations of some forms of emotion, such as love, affection, and friendship, and are encouraged to express others, such as anger, aggression, and jealousy. These manifestations are so accepted that these often become a license for violent acts.

There are studies that seek to explain the relationship between masculinity and violence by means of biology and genetics. Besides being stronger than women, genetic mutation is attributed with the capacity to manifest extremes of brutality and even sadism.

Other studies have shown that for some men, being cruel is synonymous with virility, strength, power, and status. "For some men, the practice of cruel acts is the only way to impose oneself as a man," says the anthropologist Alba Zaluar, of the Violence Research Nucleus at the Rio de Janeiro State University.

Violence against the Elderly, Children, and Black Women

Besides the Women's Police Stations (see below), the Police Station for Protection of the Elderly and GRADI (Repression and Analysis of Intolerance Offenses Group) also serve women who have suffered violence, whether they are elderly, nonwhite, homosexuals, or from any other group that is considered a "minority." In the case of violence against girls, the Police Stations for Protection of the Child and Adolescent can also be used.

In Brazil, black and native women carry the heavy burden of their history of abuse and sexual violence, having been treated for centuries as machines for sex, without any basic human rights.

Nowadays, black and native women suffer a double discrimination—both of gender and race—plus a third, that of class, with most of the women being poor. All these factors increase the vulnerability of these women, who often face violence not only outside but also inside their homes.

Women's Police Stations

In the struggle to put an end to violence against women, the setting up of the Women's Police Stations twenty years ago was the first big step in Brazil. Another big step was the creation of the special criminal courts. With their setting up, about ten years ago, the time span between an individual being accused by a woman and the accuser's trial became much shorter. The process, which before had taken years, because it was referred to the criminal courts along with thousands of others, can now be resolved in a matter of months, and the accused is kept away from the woman until the process ends. Fear and embarrassment are factors that influence the women who do not want to be identified, some young, and others who are older, rich and poor, the weak and the strong, everyone has these two feelings in common. Each one has a story and all of them are difficult to tell: 1. She began to be afraid of her husband from the time when she was sleeping and he stabbed her with a knife. 2. She woke up with her face all marked and deformed, said another victim. 3. Her husband arrived home and told her the only reason he didn't shoot her was because he didn't want to spend the money on the bullet and that she wasn't worth it, another one said. 4. Another lamented that her husband had killed everything that was good inside her.

Every fifteen seconds a woman is assaulted in Brazil. Research carried out by the Perseu Abramo Foundation revealed what happens inside Brazilian homes. And the reality makes unsettling reading. Every year, two million women are beaten by their partners, husbands, or boyfriends. Studies show that violence is often continuous but escalates gradually. If the woman begins to forgive a slap in the face, this soon becomes more violent. Aggression under control, with prevention being better than the cure: dealing with violence before it happens and not afterward when it has already marked body and soul. The idea that has been used and found to work is not to have couples living in peace, but rather getting the whole community, where five thousand families live, living in peace.

The Principal Cases Attended by the Women's Defense Police Station

Bodily injury: cases of beating, punching, slapping, kicking, and the use of sharp objects (knives, scissors, etc.).

Rape: forced sex through the use of violence or threat (forced sex between husband and wife; with mentally disabled; with minors under fourteen years of age are also considered rape).

Sexual assault: forced intimate contact, without sex.

Abduction: being taken by force or under threat to a place with the intention of having intimate contact, without sex taking place.

Threat: intimidation, by means of words or gestures, indicating the intention of doing harm.

Slander: false accusation.

Calumny: offense against honor, in the presence of others.

Insult: offense, without the presence of witnesses.

The police station also acts in cases of separation of couples, child support, separation of property, and searches for children.

What Can Be Done?

Women who suffer violence can go to any police station, but they should preferably go to the Specialized Attendance of Women Police

Stations (DEAM), also called Women's Police Stations (DDM). There are also services based in hospitals and universities that offer medical, psychological, and social assistance and legal guidance.

Women who suffer violence can also look for help from the Public Attorney services and special criminal courts, the State Councils of Women's Rights, and women's organizations.

How Complaints Work

If an incident is reported at a police station, it is important to provide a detailed statement and to take witnesses, if there are any, or to provide their names and addresses. If the woman believes that her life (or those of her family members, children, parents, etc.) is at risk, she can also seek help from organizations that have refuges, which are places kept in secret where a woman and her children can be away from the aggressor.

Depending on the type of crime, a woman may or may not require an attorney to bring a court case. If she does not have the money, the State may nominate an attorney to defend her. Often women turn back and fail to follow through with the legal action. In some cases, a woman can claim damages for losses suffered. To do this she should go to the Constitutional Rights and Damage Claims Office.

Why Do Men Beat Their Wives?

The reasons for this insane act are the starting point for the discussion. Men who assault women are not sick, only 6 percent of these men have any serious mental or emotional disturbance. If there is any disease, it is a collective cultural disease. So we cannot think of it as a group therapy for abusive men. It is not a psychological question, it is a cultural question, and this does not bring an end to domestic violence.

The Economic Cost of Domestic Violence

According to data from the World Bank and from the Inter-American Development Bank:

One in every five days off work is caused by violence suffered by women in their own homes.

A woman who suffers domestic violence sees her life expectancy decrease by one year for every five years she spends suffering domestic violence.

Rape and domestic violence are serious causes of incapacity and death of women of productive age. In Latin America and the Caribbean, domestic violence affects between 25 and 50 percent of women.

Women who suffer domestic violence generally earn less than women who do not suffer domestic violence.

In Canada, a study estimated that the costs of violence against women exceed $1 billion (Canadian) per year in services, including the police, criminal justice system, advice services, and training.

In the United States, a survey estimated the cost of violence against women between $5 billion and $10 billion per year.

According to the World Bank, in developing countries it is estimated that between 5 and 16 percent of healthy years of life are lost by women of reproductive age as a result of domestic violence.

A study by the Inter-American Development Bank estimated that the total cost of domestic violence is between 1.6 and 2 percent of GDP of a country.

Transcribed from the site http://copodeleite.rits.org.br/apc-aa-patricia galvao/home/mapadosite.shtml. Accessed in December 2009.

Chapter 8

Why Do We Accept Domestic Violence?

I could not have imagined that domestic violence caused so many deaths. Looking at the results of my research, I was horrified by what had happened to humanity. God created men and women in this world to love each other. We should pray and ask God to free us from evil temptations. I am very sorry for those that have lost their lives because of domestic violence, and I ask the good Lord to make things better. The objective of this book is to make everyone understand, especially women, that our lives are in danger if we continue to ignore the facts and do not look for specialized help.

I learned that domestic violence is any instance of psychological, economic, sexual, or physical coercion within a relationship, in which harm is deliberately caused or attempts are made to control the conduct of another person. I want to make it clear that this means not only physical aggression, as everyone thinks when talking about domestic violence, but also verbal aggression, psychological abuse, undesired sexual contact, destruction of property, harming pets, financial control, social isolation, threats or intimidation of other members of the family, and limiting access to work. The biggest victims of domestic violence are women and children, but there are cases where the victims are men.

I learned that in Argentina, it is estimated that about 25 percent of women regularly suffer from domestic violence and that 50 percent of them will experience a situation of domestic violence at some time in their lives. Although it is recognized that domestic violence is a common situation in society, this crime of violence is not part of a regular medical check-up. Why? This seems to be caused by a series of factors such as the brevity of the doctor's visit and the embarrassment of speaking on this subject to other people. So how can one recognize victims of domestic violence? By means of clinical indicators by potential victims of abuse, such as dental trauma, blows and bruises principally to the head and on the skin, cuts, fractures, burns, long and medium term abortions, chronic headaches, sexual dysfunction, chronic abdominal pain, peptic ulcers, nonspecific gastro-intestinal complaints, atypical heart pain, sleep disturbances, sexually transmissible diseases, panic attacks, alterations to eating habits, suicidal ideas, undesired pregnancies, muscular and skeletal symptoms, breathing difficulties, nausea, depression, irritability, panic attacks, feelings of insecurity, phobias, low self-esteem, insomnia, anxiety, and toxic substance abuse. The characteristics of the injuries caused by domestic violence principally to the head, face, and mouth are neurological symptoms, such as acute loss of sight or hearing. Although victims of domestic violence visit their doctors more frequently, the description of their symptoms is vague, and they are often unsatisfied with their doctors and often change them.

Medical procedures should be established to question patients in this situation, getting straight to the heart of the matter, domestic violence, avoiding judgment and adopting an attitude that encourages trust. The scholars say there are simple questions to use to be able to start a conversation with people who are going through domestic violence: Do you feel insecure at home? Has someone in your home injured you or are they treating you differently? These questions can help to successfully detect domestic violence. Other questions could be asked: Has someone tried to control you in some way? Are you afraid of your husband? If the patient admits the abuse, you can then ask for specific details, such as the date, circumstances, and results; domestic violence is considered to have a different diagnosis from other conditions related to the symptoms such as those mentioned earlier; in the clinical history, exhaustively document the report on the episode of domestic violence and also all the results of the physical examinations; discover the resources available in the community so as to be able to refer victims to multidisciplinary centers that can offer assistance.

Interdisciplinary communication between doctors, nurses, social workers, and others is of great importance to correctly and safely treat the patient. The role of the clinical doctor is also of great importance in recognizing victims of domestic violence, in giving their support and in urging regular attendance of routine examinations at the clinic. The doctor should know about the resources in their communities so they can refer their patients, and if these are not available, to have the support of other professionals such as psychiatrists and social workers so as to be able to resolve the patient's problems.

We have an example of the brutal violence against women that is the norm in Lagos, Nigeria: a typical fight between a husband and wife. She wants to visit her parents and he wants to stay at home. And so they resolved the dispute in a way that some people say is quite common: the husband beat her, as one wife recounted an incident that happened to her. The husband followed his wife to the door, beating her until she lost consciousness, and left her in the street in front of the apartment where they lived. At that time, she was thirty-one years old and had been married five years, and she broke the unwritten rule in this part of the world: she challenged her husband! Research in sub-Saharan Africa shows that many men and women consider such disobedience to be a fully justifiable reason for the administration of a beating, but that is not how this university educated woman thought. She packed her clothes and left home as soon as she got out of hospital. Although her determination weakens at times, and despite not wanting a divorce, she has not returned. "He did not believe in my own rights," she said in an interview. "If I said no, he beat me, and this is not what I wanted for my life."

Women are victims of violence in any society. In a few places, however, the practice of this type of abuse is more deeply rooted or is more accepted. One in every three Nigerian women interviewed said they had been the victim of physical abuse. The wife of the vice-governor of a northern province of Nigeria told reporters that her husband beat her unceasingly. One of the reasons for the beatings was the fact that she watched films on television. One of the people designated by the president to take part in the national commission against corruption was murdered by her husband, two days after having asked for protection from the state police commissioner. It was as if it were normal for women to be treated by their husbands as a punching bag, said one Nigerian official. The code of conduct in the Muslim-dominated north of the country is very permissive in allowing husbands to discipline their wives, as well as allowing parents and teachers to discipline children, provided that they are not seriously hurt.

Laws in relation to aggression could be applied, but the police generally see the beating of women as an exception. Legislation on domestic violence has been proposed in six of the thirty-six Nigerian provinces but has been implemented in only two of them. Activists who defend women's rights say that the prevalence of abuse demonstrate the low status of women in sub-Saharan Africa. Generally they have less education, work longer hours, and carry three times the weight that men carry when it comes to carrying firewood, water, and bags of maize.

In the book *Marriage and Slavery*, not all women fit into this pattern. The author spoke in a television interview with a confident and assertive tone of voice, and said that her diary is full of plans in relation to the various projects she intends to implement. "I am an organizer," she said, but this did not save her from the apparently unceasing beating sessions during eight years of marriage to her husband. One daughter told of her parents being progressives, that her father sometimes beat her mother, but he also encouraged his daughter, the eldest of seven, to study and later to follow a career in marketing management. She was only sixteen when she met her husband. Like her, he was at university, specializing in accountancy. Tall and slim, he only beat her once during their long period of dating, as she recounted it. She thought this was an exception to the rule, but that was not the case.

She is now thirty-five and says that her husband beat her more than sixty times after getting married in 1997, including when she was pregnant with her son, who is now six years old. He threw a flashlight at her and also a knife, which cut her head, whilst a friend begged him not to kill her. Her husband, who is now thirty-six, said that he made a mistake in beating his wife. But in a two-hour interview conducted in his office, he insisted that she deliberately provoked him; he became increasingly agitated when he remembered how she had challenged his authority.

"Can you imagine, beating my wife?" he said. "You cannot imagine being pushed to this level? But some people simply push you to your limit, and you do things you shouldn't do, by God, as a man and head of the family. As that, one needs the house to be submissive."

As far as he is concerned, that means accepting that he is the head of the household and it is he that makes all the final decisions and also means that all the property has to be in his name, and that the wife should ask permission to visit her family. When his wife started looking for help, others seemed to support her husband's position. She went to the police and they told her "he was no young boy," she remembered. They said that if she no longer wished to be married "that she should divorce him." She also asked for help from her father-in-law, who told her that "beating is normal." She also asked for help from the local church minister, and he advised her "not to upset her husband" and "to submit to everything her husband said to her."

Finally, she found support in Violence Against Women Watch, a nonprofit organization that runs two shelters in Nigeria, and she went to live there for a few weeks. Her report, which details the violence she suffered, was given the title "A Cry for Help." A leading member of staff of the organization said that the group's files document two hundred cases such as hers. Even women like her, who are economically independent, are reluctant to divorce for fear of falling into social disgrace. In this society, a woman has to do all she can to make her marriage work.

Chapter 9

A Bad Marriage Wounds the Heart

Marriage is good, but you have to be very careful about the type of person you choose. This is the advice everyone should give to their children who think they are adults at the age of fifteen. When we meet people we like, it's normal to feel butterflies in the stomach, our heart beating so hard we think it will come out of our mouth, and the desire is always to be close to that person and sometimes to suffer in silence because the other person does not even know they are loved.

But it is very important how the young man treats his girlfriend. If the young girl thinks this is her true love, she should wait and see; if the young man is aggressive, if he forbids her from having friends or going out alone, if he tells her how to cut her hair or use make-up, if he abuses her physically or verbally, if he humiliates her, if he manipulates her, if he forces her to have sex, she should not marry him. These are signs one should pay attention to when in a relationship. This advice is also good for boys, because there are also manipulative, authoritarian, jealous, exploitative, and violent girls. Love is the most marvelous thing in the world, and you should be able to enjoy it throughout your life and be happy. Love is something inexplicable and is only complete if each person respects the other.

Young people, if you come from an unhappy home, do not make the same mistakes as your parents.

Scientists and doctors say that a bad marriage brings disease, and a bad relationship can increase the risk of becoming sick.

In a study carried out by the British Civil Service, out of 9,011 participants, almost 34 percent of those who had problems in their relationship had suffered a heart attack or other types of heart problems in the twelve years of the research. In this study, the researchers were most concerned about the quality of the marriages and relationships. They confirmed that being married is, in general, a good thing, but you have to be careful what kind of person you marry.

Another author, Donald Hewlett, said that research he carried out at University College, London demonstrated that the quality of a relationship was important. He and his colleagues are conducting tests to see if the study on bad relationships shows any biological evidence that stress can contribute to heart problems, which also includes inflammation and high levels of hormonal stresses.

Another recent study looked at the quality of relationships, finding that there was no association between matrimonial ties, in general, and the risks of heart disease or premature death. But after ten years of follow-up checks, the researchers concluded that women who keep quiet in all the arguments during the marriage have an increased risk of dying younger, in comparison with those who express themselves and say what they feel when the couple fights. As for the men, the risk of dying in a bad relationship is lower, after a study that looked at almost four thousand men and women and which was published in the *Psychosomatic Medicine Journal*. In the end, both men and women who are in a bad relationship run the same risks of becoming sick or of dying early.

Individual or couple therapy is a good investment in prevention, but can one advise people who are having problems in their relationship to consider therapy? They may have other reasons for not doing it; perhaps they think it is impossible that any kind of therapy alone could prevent a heart attack. Ending a terrible relationship is not necessarily the solution, and besides that, if someone is not married, that does not mean that they run no risk of having a heart attack.

As an example, let's take the experience of a pretty woman in her early sixties. After thirty-five years of being married, she and her husband separated. Why now, after so many years together? She said that they never argued and never had any kind of physical violence, but that their relationship was silent and empty. Silence and emptiness are also symptoms that a marriage is breaking down. Marriages going defunct are a bigger threat to couples, not so much due to the presence of conflict, which kills a long-term relationship, but by the lack of affection and involvement between the couples.

But the lack of affection and intimacy between couples are not the reasons causing divorces nowadays, but rather very different ones. The number one problem in a relationship is money, with relationships sometimes breaking down solely because of this. Another is conflict due to jealousy: the man spending the night away from home or not wanting to go out with his wife because he has a lover. These are the problems that are now causing deaths rather than divorces in some couples. There are also those who, for some reason, remain married even when suffering all kinds of abuse, or because in many countries there is no divorce.

Many divorces happen in the first ten years of being married, but when people reach the age of fifty or sixty, most couples that experience conflict have already separated. After two or three decades of being married, you learn how to handle conflicts and to negotiate your differences, such as who is responsible for leaving the bathroom dirty, who always arrives late, who is more authoritarian or more easygoing with the children.

The best time to get to know one another is when we are young, because if you fight, you can make up afterward, and in the beginning you can get over the differences, and later on you just want peace and affection. There is evidence that couples who have been married longer are happier because the passions have died down with age. But one cannot always look back on having been together for twenty years or more. The children are already grown up and the couples are retired; no one is forcing anyone else to stay together. Without any strong and positive influences in the relationship, couples can begin to display the signs of tiredness.

A sixty-year-old man in Massachusetts described how he left his wife after thirty-three years together. They each had a career and separate lives. They had their own friends and even went on vacation separately. They had their differences, and after years of being married and employed, he retired, and this brought on a personality crisis. He was without work and not really emotionally involved in his marriage. The point arrived where it was too late for marriage counseling, because mentally he was already out of marriage.

In times gone past, marriage was traditionally chiefly concerned with having children and bringing them up, but now romance, love, and intimacy are the pillar of marriage; only 40 percent of married people have children, compared with 75 percent of couples in 1880, according to a study at the University of Pennsylvania. Most people who remain married for a long time are able to handle conflicts, and those who cannot, separate. Those who remain married for a very long time, or who did not give too much importance to life's duties, try to enrich their relationship, overcoming conflicts.

Chapter 10

WHY DON'T WE DIVORCE OUR ABUSERS?

Why don't women who suffer violence separate from their torturers before something awful happens? This is what some people think who have never had to live through this difficult situation (and divorce is illegal in some countries). I should explain that in some countries the law means that poor people cannot get a divorce, as happened in my case. I am married and live in New York, with two children, and I have two jobs and live with domestic violence. I have tried to get divorced several times, but the doors were closed to me because it cost a few thousand dollars. As it was difficult for me to get that kind of money, I could not get a divorce, and I remain married, living with the same man, in the same house.

Do you think that if people live with domestic violence they can find support? Just one example, if divorce cost less, they would not have to continue living with their torturers. In my case, I have suffered no physical violence and have no marks on my body, and so they think I should continue to live with my abuser. Here is another example of why it is so hard for someone to get a divorce. In Santiago, the capital of Chile, which was the last country in South America to allow divorce, the Minister of Justice thought that the divorce law was a historic step for the country and for the first woman in Chilean history to obtain a divorce. For one woman it was a great victory: she has a new life, with dignity and without fear.

When the doors of the court opened in Santiago, she was the first in line, alleging that she was abused by her husband. She had been married for twenty-five years and based her petition on the many, many years of violence she had suffered at the hands of her husband, from whom she had been separated for six months, and with whom she had two grown-up children. This law allowed her to recover her dignity and her freedom. On the other hand, the Chilean Congress, six months after passing the law, blocked the divorce law because 87 percent of the population consider themselves Catholics. Malta and the Philippines are also countries where divorce is still not legally permitted.

Chileans commemorated that day as historic for the country, but even so, people with a problem in their marriage are forced to ask for an annulment, and six thousand couples are approved every year in a country of fifteen million inhabitants. Annulment in the old legal system cost 670 pesos, when the minimum wage there was 196 pesos a month. In that country, the new law only allowed divorce after they had been separated for a year, if both partners agreed, or after three years if only one accepted the idea. There should be no need for such a wait when there is domestic violence. The law in that country means that couples have to go through marriage counseling for at least sixty days before asking for a divorce. How can people who are earning the minimum wage, sometimes with children, pay for a divorce at such a high cost?

Even if they could, how many years will pass for the person to be able to have so much money? I think that the law in any country does not help poor people to get a divorce, and this is why couples are killing each other. In New York, divorces are resolved more easily, as it is one of the states that accepts no-fault divorce, without having to involve lawyers. Despite various failings in divorce cases, these are generally the easiest cases to resolve. The lawyers allege that people can abuse the system and that the number of false marriages is increasing, exposing people's private life in public.

This situation causes much social misery and involves a lawyer who always has to ask some indiscreet questions, such as whether the couple have had sex, and if not, this means that the marriage is false, often just to be able to gain residence status in the country. To get a divorce in New York, one of the couple has to be guilty of adultery, abandonment, or physical harm. In New York, 75 percent of the 62,530 petitions for divorce were by agreement between the husband and wife. With faith in God, I hope that this law is changed in favor of women. Women have to learn that when a relationship is not working out, we should leave our partners. But this is impossible for many women, sometimes because of the love for the partner and because of the children who do not want to grow up fatherless, sometimes because they need him to put food on the table for the family, because they do not work, sometimes because they are afraid of being alone, sometimes even because they have become used to the abuse and think there is no way out.

Some Brazilian women believe 100 percent in marriage, for traditional and religious reasons, and do not care what happens between a couple, and they defend their beliefs to the bitter end. Most are independent, work and take care of the children as head of the family in all social classes, including a large portion of people on lower income, as published studies have shown. Nowadays the rate of separations and divorces has grown in many countries.

Divorces

The divorce rate in Brazil rose by 200 percent between 1984 and 2007, according to *Registration Statistics 2007*, published by the Brazilian Geography and Statistic Institute (IBGE). In this period, the rate went from 0.46 divorces per thousand inhabitants to 1.49. In absolute numbers, divorces granted went from 30,847 in 1984 to 179,342 in 2007. Considering the total of direct uncontested divorces and separations, IBGE said there were around 231,000 dissolutions, which means approximately one dissolution in every four marriages. In 2007, direct divorces, that is, divorces without any judicial separation process beforehand, represented 70.9 percent of the total. According to the study, last year, in 89 percent of divorces, the responsibility for the care of the children went to the mother. The analysis by IBGE demonstrated a rise in the rate during the period under consideration, and shows there has been a gradual change in behavior of society, which has come to accept divorce as more natural. In addition to this, there was also an increase in the demand for the services of the legal system to formalize the situation of dissolution of the marriage.

Text transcribed from the site: pe360graus.globo.com/noticias/brasil/ciencia/2008/12/04/NWS,477695,3,377, NOTICIAS,766-TAXA-DIVORCIOS-CRESCE-200-ANOS-DIZ-IBGE.aspx, published on 12.04.2008. Accessed in December 2009.

In 2007, divorce in Brazil had been legalized for thirty years, and the Brazilian Geography and Statistic Institute recorded the highest rate of marriages being dissolved in the country since birth, marriage, and death registration statistics were started in 1984. In 2007, the number of marriages continued to rise in Brazil, but instances of divorce leapt. Whereas 916,000 couples officialized their marriage last year, about 3 percent more than in 2006, almost 180,000 became divorced, a growth of 44 percent in the same period.

Introduced in Brazil in 1977, divorce has changed the ways of Brazilian families in the last three decades and has been increasingly used in recent years. In 1989, the reduction from five to two years of separation required for divorce has already doubled the rate in the country. Last year, Brazil had 1.49 divorces for every thousand adults over the age of twenty. This new rate is the result of a law that came into effect in January of last year, which allows the dissolution of the marriage in registration offices, without having to go through the justice system.

Couples without small children who agree to end their marriage can become free by simply signing their divorce papers. This was the choice of about 15 percent of those who became divorced in 2007. In 1984, Brazil had 0.46 divorces for every thousand adults. The growth over twenty-three years was of more than 200 percent. The manager of life statistics and population estimates at IBGE, Claudio Crespo, said the relative stability in the rate of separations indicates that couples are seeking the direct divorce, which accounted for almost 71 percent of the total granted in 2007.

"The ease in obtaining a divorce is leading to couples taking this step sooner, eliminating judicial and bureaucratic processes," said Crespo.

He said this could also explain the slight increase in nonconsensual separations, which account for about 24 percent of the total. "When the two agree, the couple tends to go for direct divorce," Crespo said. "The registration office divorce is yet another facility, although not yet that well known by people." About 42 percent of registration office divorces in 2007 were in the state of São Paulo.

Text transcribed from the site: www.tribunadonorte.com.br/noticia.php?id=94804, Publication: 12.05.2008. Accessed in December 2009.

Chapter 11

THE SILENCE ON DOMESTIC VIOLENCE AGAINST MEN

There are many reasons why we do not have much information on domestic violence inflicted against men, firstly because these incidents are rarer than instances of violence against women, and secondly because men are embarrassed to say that their wife or girlfriend beat them up. It took many years of education, advocacy, and support to encourage women to lodge complaints about the domestic violence they suffered, but as far as I'm aware, no action up to this time has been taken to ensure that men do the same. In-depth studies are lacking and do not accurately portray the actual number of men who suffer domestic violence in their relationships.

The idea of a man being violently abused by his wife in a chauvinistic society is unbelievable to most, because the impact of the violence is less apparent and very unlikely to attract the attention of others. If a man has a mark on his body or has a black eye, everyone would think he has had a fight with another man, or suffered an accident at work, or was playing sport with his friends. Many people are amazed that men can also suffer from domestic violence; men do not complain about it because they think no one will believe that they have been physically abused by their partner. Being called a coward or impotent can have a much stronger psychological impact on a man than on a woman; cruel words hurt, but they can hurt in different ways, and in many cases, men are affected more emotionally than physically. To humiliate a man in front of another man can be more devastating than physical violence.

Alcohol and drugs are the biggest cause of domestic violence, because intoxicated people have less control of their impulses and in general are quicker to resort to violence to solve their problems. Studies show that women who frequently physically abuse their partners are alcoholics. Some borderline personality disorders make women abusive and violent. Approximately 2 percent of all women have a borderline personality disorder. Almost 50 percent of all abuse and domestic violence against men is practiced by women who suffer from this dysfunction, which is also associated with suicidal behavior. These atypical women experience repeated episodes of depression, anxiety, frustration, and irritation, and they often attribute their behavior to the man. Their problems, mental and emotional, are the result of their own emotional insecurity, of traumas in their childhood, or the use of alcohol and drugs. They blame the men for their problems, without taking responsibility for themselves or doing something to resolve the situation. They refuse treatment and insist that it is the husband who needs treatment rather than themselves.

When the man can do nothing for them, they feel frustrated and think their husbands are doing this deliberately, leading to a breakdown in communication; the woman starts to insult the man, and when the man expresses his disapproval and tries to stop the fight, the woman becomes enraged and starts to throw things at him. He may think that it is all his fault. This risk of violence grows when the woman insults the man in front of the children, threatening his relationship with them, or she refuses to control her abusive behavior when the children are present. He controls himself because he does not want to leave the children alone with the abusive mother and because he is also afraid of what his wife will say to the children about him being a bad father.

Some scholars say that there are many women who commit harassment and abuse against their husbands. The American court, along with the criminal justice system, is trying to have this type of abuse recognized. The police are under a lot of pressure to protect women and to arrest the men. In the world where women victimize the men, in practice, the law offers no protection to men and is only trained to arrest them. Man have to be very old and defenseless for the authorities to believe that they are the victims. The men remain undecided as to how to report the abuses of their partners because they have become the protector of the person from whom they need protection; they are ashamed of being abused by women. The stereotypes of a chauvinistic and patriarchal society in which the man is always strong, the head of the family, does not cry or even show his feelings, has turned against man himself in the case of his victimization by the woman, because he is afraid of being considered weak and defenseless.

Some cases of domestic violence against men are presented here and in the following chapter.

United States of America

South Carolina

A couple were in a comfortable financial situation; the wife was lacking for nothing, and as far as everyone was concerned they seemed to be getting along very well. But nobody knew what happened behind that door. The wife arranged the death of her husband with her boyfriend so she could live off his inheritance. After the boyfriend killed her husband, they were both caught and are both behind bars.

Colorado

1. Someone called the police because a furious woman began to shout at her boyfriend in the street and then took off one of her shoes and started to hit him on the head with it, causing him to be hospitalized with serious fractures. The woman is in prison for her crime.

2. A man's belongings were stolen and destroyed, and his house was robbed multiple times; he became afraid to leave his house in the morning to return at night. He wanted to move but did not have the money. Was he a victim of gangs, addiction, drugs, or a few crazy criminals? Or was he the prisoner of a mentally unstable ex-wife and their oldest son? Or of the legal

system which is loaded against him and makes her an innocent party? He said that if he called the police, she would claim he attacked her; if he tried to defend his house or come close to her, she would call the police and he would be arrested as an abuser. This man told his story and said that he is one of the lucky ones because he has not been physically abused.

3. A retired fireman was repeatedly physically abused by his wife of five years. His wife attacked him by surprise, always using a kitchen knife or other implements from the house such as a gun. Even so, suffering his abuse in secret, he worked throughout his life until he reached retirement age. The problem is that after he retired, his income fell. When they were at home, he spent his time in his room or in the garage so as not to have to communicate with her. He says he is afraid to leave her because he is afraid she will go crazy, and there is nowhere that will offer him help or a place to stay. He has all the evidence of his wife's abuses documented during these five years, but says he doubts the authorities will believe in him. Call the police? He says absolutely not, saying he has no doubt that in front of the police, or a judge or jury, his wife will cry and lie, making them believe that he is the abuser even to the point of having him arrested.

4. When the police answered a call on domestic violence, they found a man running from door to door, asking for help because his girlfriend had stabbed him many times in their house. The police went to find her, but she had disappeared. The man was taken to hospital, where he recovered. His girlfriend was found days later and was subsequently tried and convicted for her crime.

Florida

1. A man was very happy with his wife and daughter, but his wife died, leaving him and his daughter alone. As time passed, his daughter was growing up and he thought he needed a

woman to help guide her, and so he decided to try to find happiness once again. He had already met a woman in the town where they lived. They started to go out and after some months decided to live together. At the start, everything was wonderful, everyone was very happy, and he seemed to have won the lottery; food on the table, a clean house, his and his daughter's clothes washed, and so on. But this happiness did not last long, and after a while he seemed to be waking from a dream, because from one day to the next the woman became a cold, cruel, and ferocious person. She started to argue, yell, and throw things, and when he didn't react as she expected, she took a knife and tried to stab not only him but also his daughter. He told her that everything was over; they moved to a friend's house and lodged a complaint. She was arrested and convicted of attempted murder.

Common sense considers domestic violence as a type of crime that only happens to women, but almost 30 percent of men say they have been victims of this kind of abuse, according to research published by the *American Journal of Preventive Medicine*. "Domestic violence suffered by men has been little studied and frequently this is hidden, almost as much as violence against women was ten years ago," said Robert Reid, from the Group Health Cooperative Center for Health Studies in Seattle. The researchers interviewed more than four hundred adult men by telephone and found that almost 30 percent had been victims of domestic violence at some moment in their lives. The extent of domestic violence against men is not a phenomena restricted to the United States: The Crimes Research Unit in the United Kingdom discovered that almost 20 percent of incidents were reported by male victims in 2001-2002, and that in half of these cases the abuse was committed by a woman. For the Group Health study, researchers included slaps, blows, kicks, and nonphysical abuse such as threats, disparaging or insulting remarks, and controlling behavior. The article indicated that previous studies backed up this new research and also said that men frequently refuse to use physical force to defend themselves and are not likely to report the abuse.

One of the most common myths about abuse suffered by men is that the person affected has the freedom to leave the abusive relationship. "We know that many women think it difficult to leave an abusive relationship, especially if they have children and do not work outside the home," said Reid. "What surprised us was that most of the men in situations of abuse also stay in the marriage, despite multiple episodes over many years."

Transcribed from the site http://livrepensar.wordpress.eom/2008/05/22/violencia-domestica-contra-os-homens/, published by Henrique Miranda, 05.22.2008. Accessed in February 2010.

Chapter 12

CASES OF MEN MURDERED BY THEIR WOMEN

Various cases of men being murdered by their girlfriends, fiancées, wives, and lovers are given here. Some of them are because they got tired of being abused or because, at that moment, it seemed to be the only solution to their problems. There are good and bad people of every sex, race, age, religion, and social class.

United States of America

Arizona

A woman who drank a lot and used a lot of drugs tied up her boyfriend and stabbed him multiple times. Her lawyer said she showed symptoms of being crazy, because she drank his blood and said she thought she was a vampire. She was sentenced to ten years in prison for her crime.

California

1. A woman had been married for more than twenty-five years; her husband worked whilst she looked after the house, and she seemed to be on very good terms with the neighbor. Her daughter, who was already a young lady, once surprised her mother being intimate with the neighbor, and when she asked her mother to explain what was going on, the mother became very aggressive and slapped her in the face. Infuriated,

the daughter told her father that her mother was cheating on him. She denied everything the daughter said and tried to pretend how much she loved her husband. She started taking care of him like never before, preparing extravagant dinners, and when he got home he was received with hugs and kisses because she was supposedly trying to improve their relationship. But it was all show; little by little she was poisoning her husband; every day she gave him a pill, saying that it was to improve his ardor, and the innocent man took it. One day, before going to work, she went with him to the car, and he said he was not feeling well because of the pills, but she told him not to worry, that it would pass. This was the last time they spoke, because that very day, he was taken to hospital in pain and had died. She accepted his death as if it were normal, because she knew what she had done, but her daughter was very suspicious. She called the police, who went to her house and listened in to the mother talking with the neighbor, saying how she had killed her husband and wanted to take everything that was his. Thanks to the bravery of the daughter, the mother and her lover are paying for the crime they committed.

2. When a wife arrived home, she found the dead body of her husband and lots of rose petals strewn over him, like the scene from the film *America Beauty*. Everyone believed her when she said her husband had taken pills from two of her prescriptions, and the case was accepted as suicide. But his family and friends could not believe he had taken his own life and asked the police to investigate further. In his body they found a huge amount of the medication fentanyl, which had disappeared from the doctor's office where she worked. She was romantically involved with her boss. It was also discovered that on the day that her husband died, she had bought roses at a food store. The jury did not spend a long time deliberating, and she was sentenced to life imprisonment.

3. For four years a couple had lived happily in Hollywood, and the woman said these were the best days of her life. The two

of them were everything a man and woman could be for each other, and she also said he was her best friend. But one day she called the police to their house, and they found the dead body of her boyfriend, shot with a .22 caliber revolver. She told the police the revolver had gone off accidentally, when he was trying to show her how to safely use a gun. Not everyone believed her, but the sentence at the trial was homicide through negligence, and she only got thirty days in prison, not thirty years.

4. Another couple lived in Hollywood, and she went to mass in an impeccable dress, and her husband would wear an elegant suit and tie. Later, in Milan on business, an unidentified man shot him twice in the back and again in the face. The police did not have to go far to find a suspect. His widow, the mother of their two daughters, was accused of paying a friend to kill her husband. She was sentenced to twenty-six years in prison.

5. A couple met each other when they were young. They lived in Hollywood and went to college together, after which they decided to get married and went to live in a small apartment. This happiness lasted for two years, and then one day the woman called 911, in desperation, saying that her husband had tried to commit suicide. Over the phone, the operator taught her how to give mouth to mouth resuscitation until the ambulance arrived. He was taken to hospital, but unfortunately, an hour later, he died. The police searched the whole of the house and found no sign of him having committed suicide; they carried out an autopsy on the body and found two types of drugs in his blood system. The victim's brother said that his sister-in-law used to have a serious drug problem. He discovered that she and a friend of hers had arranged to poison her husband in order to claim the money from his life insurance policy. The two of them are now paying for the murder with a life sentence.

Georgia

1. The husband thought there was no problem, but his wife married him for his money; wasting no time, she hired two men to kill him. They shot the poor man and later abandoned his car, containing his body, in a place far away from where the couple lived. The three were convicted and given a life sentence.

2. A man worked as a fireman and had an accident, and he had to spend a long time in hospital. His life was never the same, and it changed a lot when he met a woman and married her. He was in love with her, happy, and they had two children. Their friends thought he had changed a lot after getting married. After a few years, he began to go downhill so fast that one of his friends became worried and went to visit him at his house and found him unconscious on the floor. The friend helped him to get up and then called an ambulance, which took him to hospital. He complained of dizziness and weakness, was unable to stand up, felt a lot of pain in his stomach, and was very confused. After a few hours, he died in hospital, and his family and friends could not believe what had happened, as the doctor said his death was of natural causes. Everyone tried to come to terms with the situation, and then his mother received a letter from someone who had gone through the same pain. She explained in the letter that her son had died a few years ago with same symptoms as he had, and that coincidentally, he had been married to the same woman. The two mothers got together to talk and look for answers. The mother who had sent the letter began to talk about her son, saying he was a policeman and that after he had been married, he started to suffer from pain, dizziness, and confusion and had subsequently died.

    The doctor also said that his death was natural, but she had never believed it. She said that his wife had received $150,000 in insurance money for the death of her son. From the second husband, because he had taken her name off the insurance policy, she only had been able to receive $30,000 to pay off their debts. It was later discovered that she had killed the two of them by putting antifreeze in their food, in juices, in jelly, and in their sandwiches.

Kansas

A woman was married to a bank manager, and everything seemed fine to the neighbors, until one day they heard shots. The wife knocked on their door, crying and saying that two men had entered her house and killed her husband. At first, everyone thought she was telling the truth, but it was a lie, in fact it was murder. The wife was in love with someone else, and they had arranged to kill him, believing that this was the only way for them to be together. This case took twenty years to be solved, and they are now paying for their crime.

Maryland

The superintendent of a golf course was found dead in his bed, burned. His wife told the police that after getting drunk, they had had an argument, and to cool his head he had taken the car and had driven for hours. The police found her story hard to believe because, in the toxicological test, no trace of alcohol was found in the husband's blood, and he had stopped breathing long before the fire started. Later on, the police found out that she was with a lover, and since her husband had refused to divorce her, she had told her best friend that she was planning to kill him with an injection that would make him stop breathing. She was arrested at her friend's house, where she tried to kill herself with sixty Xanax pills. The police arrived in time to stop her, and she is now serving a life sentence.

Michigan

A young girl of just eighteen left her parents' home because her father drank a lot and beat her mother. She went to live with her sixteen-year-old boyfriend, who had his own car and spent all his time racing around, always going from one job to the next. He also drank a lot and was always taking it out on her by beating her. She became pregnant four times, which was hard on her, and he abused her until the day the children were born. Sometimes he beat her for hours, and then he would go to the bar to drink, and after a few hours, he would come home and start beating her all over again. She said she had learned not to defend herself as she was afraid he would become even more violent, and also that she thought of killing herself, but was worried who would take care of her children, and that they would never find anyone who would love them like their own mother. Millions of things went through her head because she could not take any more of his abuse, until after fourteen years of humiliation and beatings, when he returned home, as always drunk, he was so drunk that he lay down and slept. She took a gallon of gasoline, threw it all over the bed where he was sleeping, lit a match, threw it on the bed, and fled, letting the fire consume all her torment. Before the police and the fire brigade could arrive, she drove to the police station and told the policemen, "I did it, I did it." She was tried and found not guilty.

Mississippi

A couple had gotten married very young; he became a doctor and they had a daughter. Time passed and they got older, and the husband found a younger woman who worked with him in the hospital. Everything was fine until one day the phone rang in their house and the husband answered. When he finished talking, he took his revolver and left, and his wife ran out after him shouting his name and trying to take the revolver from his hand. She was accidentally shot, surviving a few days in the hospital but then died. After a year, he married his girlfriend, and they went off to live their life. Everything was going fine until he found out that his new wife was spending his money extravagantly. He started to feel unwell, his diabetes was getting worse, and he was also on the waiting list for a new liver, with his new wife appearing on a television program asking the public to help her husband with the transplant. But secretly she was poisoning him little by little, having swapped the bottle containing insulin for his diabetes with another bottle containing a different medication, and he subsequently died. Her lawyer tried to say that he had committed suicide, but his daughter said she didn't care what anyone said, her father had not killed himself, his death was murder, and the murderer was his own wife. The woman had been married before to a much younger man and had received $80,000 from his insurance. What led to her imprisonment was the falsification of the signature on the life insurance policy. Found guilty, she was given a life sentence.

Nevada

In Las Vegas, a man had been married five times; he was a man who loved women and loved to drink, but his fifth and final wife was very jealous. He was not an aggressive man, but when he drank his personality changed, according to his fourth wife. His new wife's jealousy became an obsession; she placed cameras in the house and in the office where he worked. She was hypocritical because, despite her own jealousy, she had a secret lover. One day the husband failed to show up at work, and one of his employees called the police, and the wife treated the situation as something normal, as if he had gone on vacation for a few days. When his body was found, he had already been dead for days; his body had been burned and they were only able to identify his remains thanks to one of his ex-wives, who recognized the diamond bracelet he was wearing; she had given it to him on his birthday. It took many years to prove that the current wife had anything to do with the murder of her husband, but this was confirmed, and she was given a life sentence.

New Hampshire

In Hampton, one of the pupils had a crush on the school administrator, who was twenty-two years old and married. The administrator invited the fifteen-year-old boy to visit her at her house when her husband was away. They sat down to watch TV, and then she got up and did a striptease, and they ended up having sex. She told her innocent lover that her husband was no longer functional as a man and that she wanted to take him for everything he had. Involved and with his head full of her lies, he agreed to do what she wanted and borrowed a gun. She planned everything for the night when she had a meeting at school and would be out of the house until late. She warned the boy not to kill her husband in front of the dog, so as not to traumatize the creature. One night, the boy and his friend forced the husband to kneel down and then shot and killed him. The young boys disappeared, and when the wife came home, she made a big fuss, waking up the whole neighborhood, saying that someone had killed her husband. The police had difficulty in resolving this case, until someone said that they had overheard the boys talking about this murder. The boy had recorded the conversation when the woman was arranging to have her husband killed. She was given a life sentence and the boys got twenty-eight years in jail.

New York

1. A woman whose marriage was experiencing difficulties waited until her husband was asleep at night, cut off his private parts with a knife, and threw it into the street. Thank God this was recovered and sewn back on.

2. A girl lived with her abusive boyfriend, and being tired of so much abuse, she decided to cook his favorite dish and put in enough poison to kill him. She called the ambulance, saying that her boyfriend had blacked out, but when they arrived it was confirmed that he had been poisoned.

3. Another woman lived with her boyfriend in their apartment, and they were constantly fighting. The police had been called seventeen times because of the problems they had almost. The last time the police came, they found the man with many burns, as the woman had thrown kerosene all over his body and set him alight. He was taken to hospital in critical condition.

4.   A husband and wife were at home talking about retirement and what the future held for the two of them, but they were interrupted by the phone ringing. It was one of the husband's lovers wanting to be with him. As men always know how to get around women, he told his wife in a natural way that he was going out, took his things, and left. A few hours later, when he returned home, he found his wife shot in the back four times. At first, the police suspected the husband, a thirty-nine-year-old man who was an elementary school teacher in Westchester. After a lot of investigation, the police arrested his lover, a very elegant twenty-six-year-old, with whom he had just finished their romance. Full of rage, after the phone call, she had waited for him to leave, knocked at the door, and murdered his wife. After she had done this, she even went out with him for drinks, and they had had sex in her car. The murderer's sister said that she always went out with men who were already in a committed relationship and who had large insurance policies, and that she behaved obsessively toward them, and that she had been involved with an assistant professor in Michigan. This was her biggest problem, because she was given a court order to stop going after him and his fiancée, but that was not enough, and they had had to move away. She also said that her sister was a very persistent woman and that it was impossible for her to accept rejection. The husband of the dead woman was also lacking in dignity, because after her death he continued with his lovers, this time with a very young teacher. But he received his punishment: all her relations signed a petition, and he was dismissed from the school. His murdering lover is serving a twenty-five-year prison sentence.

5.   A woman was administrator of a school for girls in Virginia, and she drove for five hours to get to New York to meet the man who had been her lover for fourteen years, the author of *The Complete Scarsdale Medical Diet*. As time passed, he felt that their relationship was cooling down, but this was no indication, on her visit she was making to him, that she should do him the kindness of the bringing her beloved a bunch of

flowers and also a .32 caliber revolver hidden in her purse. Afterward, when the cleaning lady arrived, she found the man dead with four bullets in his body. In her statements, the murderer said she planned to commit suicide, but when she found a nightdress of another woman who was much younger than her, divorced with two children and who was making him very happy, she had a fit of rage and killed him. She also said that, after she saw that he was seriously wounded, she pulled the trigger to commit suicide, but she had used the last bullets on him. The gun used in the crime was found in her car.

6.   A woman whose husband had left her for a neighbor many years ago decided to administer justice with her own hands. Without thinking properly about the stupid thing she was going to do, she paid a man $15,000 to kill her rival and also her ex-husband. Her wish was fulfilled and the two were brutally murdered. The two murderers were convicted and given life sentences.

7.   A couple with a daughter got a divorce, and despite breaking up, everything seemed to be amicable between them. However, the wife did not want to lose custody of the daughter and hired her own uncle to kill her ex-husband. One day when her husband was in the park with his daughter, the man appeared and killed him in front of her. It was thought that the wife was innocent, but after the investigation she was proven to be involved in the crime. She was given a life sentence.

8.   This case took place in Yonkers. A man and woman met when he had asked her for a cigarette; five months later, she became pregnant with his daughter. He always gave her lots of love and affection, was very solicitous and loving, but things began to change after the daughter was born. He started to go out, and the wife suspected he had another woman, but she dismissed her fears as she thought he was under a lot of pressure. He lad had to earn a living for the family, and he was only twenty-one years old. He spent all day working, and when he got home he

even helped take care of the baby. Everything had happened so quickly between them, and she understood why he would want to go back to being that boy of before, to go out with friends to have fun. She said she did not hate him, and that was why she offered him a divorce, but he always came back to see his daughter. In the fall, he decided to enter the army, and his family and friends celebrated, but not the wife; she knew that he wanted a better life and that this was his way of getting it, but she thought he could have solved things without taking this drastic step. After he left, they communicated every day, and he spoke to their daughter. The wife heard stories that he was seeing someone else and said that enough time had elapsed; she too was trying to get on with her own life and went out with another person, but every time he would return, they would get back together because she loved him, and with every call from him, she hoped they would build the family she had always wanted. Her friends always asked why she wasted her time on him, and she answered that she loved him, that he was her husband and he loved their daughter. One day, she called him as her daughter was asking after him and didn't want to go to bed without seeing him. They talked for a long time, and he told her he was going to a bar and that he would call her later; she didn't think that was a good idea but didn't say anything. A few hours later the phone rang; it was from his phone number, but it was not him speaking. It was a sergeant that knew him, who said that he had been in an argument with his ex-girlfriend, a twenty-three-year-old woman who worked in the same company as he did. She had stabbed him, and he was dead. The wife could not believe it, she thought that his friend was joking, but he wasn't. The woman was found later by the police and was arrested. The wife said that she loved her husband a lot and that everyone makes mistakes; perhaps he had made more than he should have. He paid dearly for it.

Pennsylvania

1. A woman was married but left her husband for unknown reasons. After some time, she met another suitor and within three months they were married. They were on their honeymoon and decided to go hunting; he did not like the idea but did as she wanted. At the place where they went hunting were the ex-husband with his new girlfriend and she took her ex's rifle, hid herself, and waited until her current husband went hunting, and from far away, fired one, two, and then three shots. The first shot grazed his leg, the second hit him in the arm, and the last in his back, killing him. At first it was thought to be an accident, but when they started to investigate, it was found to be a murder done by his own wife. It took five years to be discovered, but justice was done and she is in prison, paying for her crime.

2. A young man lived with his family and friends in an exemplary relationship. He was in love with a widow whose husband had died in a car accident, and they had a daughter who was now four years old. He thought this was love and his family were very happy for him and accepted the marriage. Everything was prepared and they were married. After two months, he took out a life insurance policy for $300,000, and after that, things began to change between them. They no longer got on, so much so that he commented to his sister that he regretted having got married. In the meantime, he started to feel unwell, and he was taken to hospital in a lot of pain. Tests were carried out, but nothing was found that could explain the sudden illness. As he was feeling very bad, he was given medication to relieve the pain and sent home. A few days later, the pain got worse and other symptoms appeared, such as vomiting, hallucinations, and loss of hair. This caught the attention of a doctor who started to investigate his case more closely, discovering that he had thallium in his blood system, which is rat poison. Someone was poisoning him little by little. They began investigating at the laboratory where he worked but nothing was found, then his friends were investigated, and

again, nothing was found. The doctor thought he would not survive, such a young man. Sad and in despair, his family began to suspect his wife and asked the authorities to investigate. With no suspicion in his mind, he asked for tests to be carried out on her and her daughter, to see if they too were affected with thallium, and a little poison was found in their systems, but not sufficient for them to be in any danger. And so the family wanted to know who was doing the killing and the police were involved. When they investigated the wife, she herself confessed she had started to put rat poison in his tea more than two months ago, always increasing the dose. Worst of all is that on the day he died, the whole family was present, including his father. She confessed everything in detail and was given twenty years in prison for her crime.

Tennessee

1. A woman married the minister of her church, and three children came of this marriage. She was always the victim of domestic violence and confessed that the husband abused her sexually and physically. Not wanting to suffer any more, she shot her husband in the back inside the church and killed him. She told the judge that it was an accident, but she was sentenced to many years in prison.

2. A lawyer was forever beating his wife, and she asked for police protection. He had two daughters from a previous marriage, and they all lived together. One day, as usual, they were arguing and he threatened to kill her with a gun. It is not known how, but she got the gun in her hand and he tried to take it back. The revolver went off accidentally and the bullet hit him in his jaw. Terrified and not knowing what to do, she called 911 and the paramedics declared him dead. The case went to court, but she was found not guilty.

Texas

1. A husband and wife were forty-four years old and had a good life, including a four-year-old child. She did all she could to be the perfect wife in his eyes, including having liposuction and breast implant operations. One day, she drove to a hotel to confirm her husband's infidelity, something she had suspected for a long time. She saw him leaving the elevator with his lover and started punching him, but they were separated by the doorman. She left the hotel and the husband followed her to her car; she got in, switched on the engine, and started to run him over until he fell down, then she got out of the car and went to see if he was all right. He wasn't, he was dead, and she was charged with murder. The jury asked themselves if she had intentionally killed him or if she didn't know what she was doing at that moment. The in-laws were at her side, praying she would only get a few years in prison so that she could take care of their young child, saying they wanted what was best for the family. But the court sentenced her to twenty years in prison.

2. A woman with two children was engaged to be married, but she was very stressed out, as she had to do everything alone, and she decided to commit a terrible crime. Neighbors heard shots fired and called the police; when they went to her house, they found her fiancé, who she had shot and killed; inside the house they found the bodies of the two children, who she had also murdered, and then they found her body. She had killed herself. This was a huge tragedy.

3. In Dallas a couple seemed to live well with their two children. She was a teacher and in her free time helped at the church that they went to; he often traveled on business, and when he came home from one of these trips, he found his wife dead. He was interrogated by the police, who found nothing against him, but they discovered that he had been having an affair with one of his wife's friends. She confessed she had gone to

the dead woman's house, and the wife had asked her if she was her husband's lover. She had answered that it had happened many years ago, but it was all over between them. She said she went into the garage, took an axe, and murdered the wife in her own house. Found guilty, she is paying for her crime in prison.

4. A man was born into a poor family but had always dreamt of becoming very successful. He grew up and fell in love for the first time, married, and they had two children. His dream was realized because he became the owner of a large company, and they were married for forty years, until she died of cancer. He took it so hard that he sold his company, earning more than $40 million. He started to live his life once again, traveling and having fun, and he met a woman who worked in a restaurant, whom he found very attractive. There was twenty years difference in their ages, and she also had two daughters from another partner, but they married and he adopted her daughters. He gave his new wife $500,000, which she spent in six months, but after some time she went back to going out with her ex, went out alone with friends, celebrating birthdays and the graduation of her daughters, but the husband was not there because he was not invited, even though the parties were all financed with his money. His wife hired someone to kill him, and she shot him in the stomach. He was hospitalized and recovered, but subsequently he got an infection in the cut and died. His wife and her lover were convicted and are paying for their crime.

Virginia

The daughter of a millionaire was having a romance with a man who had nothing and was transformed from a poor man into a rich man in the "horse" state. He was very popular, and everyone thought he was a good person, but he was a great womanizer, and rumors began circulating that he was cheating on his girlfriend. Her jealousy led her to the extreme of killing him, and she was arrested by the police, but not for long, as three witnesses spoke in her defense, accusing her ex of domestic violence and saying that she had shot him in self-defense. She was tried and sentenced to two months, paid a $2,500 fine, and left court a free woman.

Washington

1. A woman grew up with the ambition of becoming a millionaire; she married a doctor and had two children. After some years problems, started to arise and her husband had an affair with a nurse in the hospital where he worked. When his wife found out, she was furious and he had to move out. With all this disappointment, she began to study to be someone in life through her own efforts, and she began working. After some months, the husband returned and tried to fix the marriage. At this time, a great opportunity came up for her to work at one of the largest companies in Washington, and they bought a big mansion in one of the most exclusive parts of the city. It was not everyone who could buy a mansion like that one, but they could because everything was going just fine between them. The husband progressed as a doctor, and she rose quickly in this company and became very ambitious, craving more and more money. At this time, she had an opportunity to run for governor of Virginia, and she invested a lot of money in her campaign. During the campaign, some thieves brutally murdered her father in New York. When she got back from the funeral, she resumed her campaign again, but there were rumors that she had not been a good daughter. When polling day arrived, she lost the election, and this woman was transformed into a demon. She starting to speak badly about the winning candidate, and he in turn claimed that she had stolen millions of dollars from her company. She went crazy and hired a man to kill the new governor and her husband, but things really went badly for her, because the hit man told the police and agreed to set her up. She left him part of the

money and then went off happily to play golf as if nothing had happened. Afterward, the guy called to say that he had the money and ask if she wanted him to go ahead with the contract, and when she said yes, she was arrested right there in the club. Everyone was very surprised; no one could believe she was capable of doing something like that. She was found guilty and was given a short prison sentence. She is now free and lives under a completely different name, waiting for her next victim.

2. Every night a woman gave her husband some Excedrin tablets for his arthritis; he would kiss her and go to sleep, saying that he loved her. At six in the morning, she would get up and get ready for another day of work; she was assistant to a bank vice president. As always, before leaving she took two Excedrin tablets. One day her fifteen-year-old daughter came looking for her and found her in the bathroom, lying on the floor. She called the ambulance, and they took the mother to hospital, where she was declared dead, leaving the family traumatized by what had happened, principally because they knew she had been poisoned. The Excedrin she had taken had been swapped for a deadly poison. No one knows how her husband had survived the previous night with the same medication. What his wife had taken was not Excedrin, it was cyanide. But the couple had a neighbor who was a bit crazy. She was forty years old and lived with her second husband, who was fifty-two. The slightly crazy neighbor had divorced her first husband and married the second one because she was short of money. Then she had the idea of killing her husband and making it look like an accident to receive $105,000. One day, he got home tired from work and suffering from a headache; she gave him four Excedrin, which he took, and he started to feel sick, saying he was going to pass out. He was taken to hospital and died a few hours later. When the time came for the woman to claim the money, she was not allowed, because her husband had died of pulmonary emphysema. What had happened was that she had killed her husband and it seems the

neighbor too, because the poison was the same. Perhaps she wanted to get the woman's husband? Were they in it together? No one knows.

Other Countries

Brazil

1. A woman was married for twenty-five years with five grown-up children and a husband who was retired from the police. One of their daughters bought some painkillers to put the father to sleep, and then her mother beat her husband until he was dead. Trying to cover up the crime, she cut up the body into more than a hundred pieces, then put the pieces into different plastic bags and deposited them in trash bins, which had been put out ready for collection. Parts of the body were found by a ten-year-old child, but among the parts not yet found were the hands and head. Which seems to have been an attempt by the person who committed the crime to make identification of the victim difficult. But the wife confessed everything and her motives are still not known. She is in prison.

2. This other case happened in a small town in the interior of the country. A poor man lived there, cut off from the world because, through bad luck, he had lost both legs in an accident. But anything can happen in life as God works in special ways, and a miracle happened to this man. One day he tried his luck on the lottery and won the biggest prize, and his life was turned around. Everything changed for him, he even got a wife, something he had never had. This is what money can do. However, his fortunes took a turn for the worse, because this woman, who had sworn eternal love not for his personality, but rather for his money, also had a lover, and together the two of them murdered the poor man for his money. Thank God, they were captured and are now serving life sentences.

Mexico

A woman was tired of suffering from her husband's violence. Every day after drinking, he would come home drunk and beat her over nothing. She decided to put an end to this abuse, and when he attacked her again, she tied up his hands, picked up a knife, and stuck it in his neck, leaving him to bleed to death. The woman was arrested and is awaiting sentencing.

Chapter 13

DOMESTIC VIOLENCE ALSO AFFECTS HOMOSEXUALS

What is domestic violence between persons of the same sex? Domestic violence in a relationship is a question of power and control between the individuals concerned, and this pattern of behavior also occurs in homosexual relationships. Domestic violence is nothing more than the exercise of power and control over one's partner: any act of physical, emotional, psychological, or material abuse, as well as the destruction of property. Domestic violence takes place in any intimate relationship and includes not only the abuses already mentioned, but social isolation, threats, intimidation, sexual abuse, economic abuse, and many other more sophisticated forms of abuses.

Homosexuals who abuse their partners often take advantage of society's homophobia as a weapon: threatening to disclose their sexual orientation to their family, friends, employers, or churches; saying that no one will help the victim because the legal and police system is homophobic or believes that homosexuals do not abuse; or by saying that the victim deserves to be abused because they are homosexual and different. Sometimes the abuser tries to convince their partner that their abusive behavior is normal and that other people do not understand their relationship.

In Western Australia, a gay man killed his partner with a knife after fourteen years of living together, and he claimed self-defense. He said he had been physically, sexually, and emotionally abused by his partner over many years. The jury found the accused man innocent, and this was the first case in Australia with such a result.

In couples of the same sex, the person who suffers from domestic violence is often the one who plays the submissive, "feminine" role. Domestic violence between partners of the same sex reflects the parameters of heterosexual relationships, including prejudices such as chauvinism. The men are forced to face this heterosexual stereotype in the definition of masculinity, in which aggressiveness and dominance are venerated as the characteristics of a man. If the man is violent and controls the relationship with the other man, this is acceptable to them. In recent years, domestic violence has been growing and is predominant in heterosexual relationships, but it has also grown in homosexual relationships.

The discussion on domestic violence in Australia seems to assume that domestic violence is something that occurs only in the heterosexual community. The absence of any reference to domestic violence among same sex couples demonstrates this. There was never much interest in the problem of domestic violence between persons of the same sex; if there was it would be the ideal opportunity to call attention to the question, but unfortunately this opportunity was allowed to pass and silence descended, which reflects very badly on society.

It is said that lesbians become involved in abusive relationships due to too much power, copying heterosexual relationships. All lesbians are different, and some may behave violently toward their partners, just like some men. The Gay and Lesbian Counseling Service (GLCS) provides advice and support to persons of the same sex suffering from domestic violence, and they depend on volunteers to provide telephone counseling and information services to homosexuals. Counselors receive training in many areas, including domestic violence.

Between the police and the United States courts there is every reason for homosexuals who are victims of domestic violence to put their hopes in these institutions, because they have the right to be protected by the law, without suffering any discrimination. To this end, an education program should be implemented in these legal institutions to teach people about homophobia and domestic violence. Some progress has been made by the police in dealing with domestic violence in the gay community, but much more is needed. Support services and special programs for couples of the same sex who suffer from domestic violence are limited. Homosexuals suffering domestic violence have the right to receive legal assistance and support, including suitable shelters, because while some shelters are responsible and sensible in catering for their needs, many do not.

In Portugal, a study at the University of Minho concluded that incidences of violence between homosexual couples are higher than incidences between heterosexuals. Despite its invisibility, violence in homosexual relationships "tends to be higher." This study found that 39.1 percent of participants admitted to having behaved with violence and 37.7 percent said they had been victims of at least one act of abuse in the last year.

"The sample is small and specific," pointed out Carla Axe, coauthor of the study with Laura Gil Costa and Rute Antunes. There were 151 individuals who responded to the survey; 37.7 percent were students and 19.9 percent had intellectual and scientific professions; the study also found that people "with a higher level of education tend to identify behavior as violent that is trivialized by the less well educated."

These professors said that violence between couples of the same sex had been "denied or hidden" by the homosexual community, which reinforced negative stereotypes, and by researchers in the area, as they question the feminist premise that violence is the child of gender inequality. Questions of gender "are relative" as they are "associated with differences in power and the differences in power occur irrespective of gender."

As in heterosexual relationships, "the victim feels isolated, vulnerable, imprisoned in the relationship." They are imprisoned by love and by financial factors. There is, however, one "important difference": prejudice.

Web of Silence

Various myths help to build the web of silence. Axe said society tends to see "homosexual relationships as egalitarian" and "immune from intimate violence," as if their relationships were "merely sexual."

Multiple studies have suggested that homosexuals are "deeply discriminated against in various sectors of society." This discrimination occurs in the family, in access to work and housing, in jobs, in schools, in the police, in the army, and in other institutions. They may "feel they are against the world—and this feeling may feed the relationship, but it can also make it more tense," Axe explained.

Homophobia can generate "low self-esteem or feelings of sexual inadequacy which the person may seek to compensate through subjugation of the partner." It may also "function as a legitimization of the violence suffered, as the individual believes they deserve it or even blame themselves for the violence."

Homosexual victims as a rule have less support. Sometimes their families do not even know they are in a relationship. Revealing the violence may also be seen as a way of reinforcing the negative image the family has of homosexuality. Axe concluded that victims may even prefer "to stay in a violent intimate relationship than to allow comments along the lines of I told you so."

Transcribed from the site www.publico.pt/Sociedade/violencia-entre-casais-homosexuais-e-maior-do-que-nos-heterosexuais_1391381. Accessed in February 2010.

Chapter 14

DOMESTIC VIOLENCE AMONG THE LOW-, MIDDLE-, AND HIGH-INCOME SOCIAL CLASSES

I collated all my research about domestic violence. Before, I could not have made any kind of comment about any kind of violence, much less domestic violence, but thanks to the media, principally television, I learned that it does not matter which social class we are from, families at all levels of income suffer from violence of all kinds.

In earlier times, due to the lack of money and education and the patriarchal culture that still permeates our society, generally the man was the only one who worked to sustain the family and the woman stayed at home, taking care of the children. Nowadays, this situation has changed because many women work, and they still take care of the family and the man as well. However, husbands often treat their wives as property; he thinks that he can beat her and abuse her as much as he wants, and the woman accepts this due to financial need, because she needs him to support her and her children, or through ignorance because she thinks she cannot continue without a man.

In modern life, with the progress in women's struggle for gender equality, sexual freedom, and financial independence, things are getting better. Before a woman becomes involved with a man, she should think of getting an education and working, trying to find out a little about everything; she should not allow domestic violence to continue: at the first sign she should get out, be financially and emotionally independent of the man. I observed that, principally among poor families, the men became involved with many women, went out with multiple women, slept with multiple women, and did not have the time to pay due attention to their own family, much less to others. It is not just having a good job and financially being able to keep many women, everyone needs care and dedication.

There are women who fight for men of this kind, many prostitute themselves, take drugs, and get drunk to steal from the wallets of other men, mostly to be able to keep their partners who exploit them. But there are also many cases of serious women who keep their family and whose partners are violent toward them and who exploit them. There are also those women who do horrible things to their newborn children, selling them to be able to buy drugs for themselves and their lovers, and others who use their own children to make a living at their expense. I see children eating trash; many of them die after being poisoned from the trash. I see children sleeping in the street, I see children selling candy and snacks, I see children prostituting themselves just to make a living, and many of them come from families living with domestic violence, some of them being turned out of their own house by their own parents.

I knew a family in which the husband not only beat his wife but also his children, and the worst of it is that he tried to kill everyone. He would not allow his son to have contact with his own mother, and this meant that the boy disappeared from home and went to live in the street, living under a bridge for a year. I cannot understand why these mothers do not fight to defend their children. Principally in the lowest income class, women should have more courage, not allowing themselves to be manipulated by their partners. After so much abuse and violence, they even open their mouths to say they still love their partners. Where is their own pride and personal dignity?

Why do they not try to defend themselves? We are human beings worthy of respect, and we, the women, are the ones who become pregnant and live nine months with a new being in our bellies; we deserve all the consideration in the world, and our children deserve a better future. But there is also love and understanding in many families of the lowest income social class, where the parents work hard to give their children a better future, and these children make the most of these opportunities.

In speaking of violence in the middle-income social class, I have watched the news from many parts of the world for almost thirty years. I was surprised to see that there is domestic violence throughout the world and in all social classes, and at least where I live here in the United States, most of the cases take place in this class, where it gets to the point of the boyfriends, fiancés, husbands, and lovers taking the lives of their partners, and I ask myself why.

In these news programs I have watched, I reached the conclusion that in the lowest income social class there is much more physical violence but fewer fatalities.

In the middle-income social class, most women work, sometimes in two or three jobs, and they also do all the housework, doing double and triple tasks. I believe there is a lot more domestic violence in this class than in the low-income sector. Why is this? Many men and women come to the United States from other countries, knowing what poverty is and wanting to overcome all the misery they have gone through, struggling for a better life here. They want to meet new people, believe they are better off here, and do everything possible so that the abuse they suffered in their countries will not happen again here, but often this is not the case.

First, some men begin by manipulating their women with lies; they do not want them to have friendships, do not want them to go out with their friends, do not want them to open their eyes, and also separate them from their own families. I have gone through this and am a little better informed about domestic violence. Financially, they may be better off in this country, but their hearts continue to suffer. What can we do? Did God make us to give a lot of love to the men we love and to the children born of this love, and is it only us who sacrifice ourselves for them, often paying with our own lives?

These questions are generally asked by people from the middle and upper classes because things are easier for them financially, but even in the middle classes, there are difficulties that make it hard to resolve the problem of domestic violence. In America, it is easier to have what we want, things we never had in the past, for example, if we want to buy a car, this process does not take as long as a month, nor one week, not even one day, sometimes it is a question of a few hours, and buying the house of our dreams is much easier, and there is no shortage of work. Many couples have separate bank accounts. I believe that each one should have their own bank account, as then everyone has the right to do what they like with their money, after fulfilling the obligations to maintain the house and support the children.

Many men in this country are cold and lazy, and they have a kind of machismo that destroys all our love for them. However, in spite of the violence, we women are defending ourselves more. Many, many women are seeking help and are becoming more independent, both financially and emotionally, even sexually, because we may think we need a man for love and sex, but there are products sold in stores that offer personal satisfaction. I thank God and the people who invented the sex shop; I bought a false penis, what a wonder! I use it whenever and wherever I want, I choose the size and width, it is always hard when needed, I can put it in any position, I am not infected with any type of disease, I am not rejected, I have sex as many times as I want, and best of all, I do not have to run to the bathroom to wash myself.

Women think that we need men to give us these kind of pleasures, but I am very happy with this experience and recommend any woman to try out these pleasures of life. Another thing I discovered is that many women, after having gone through so much violence, seek other kinds of relationships, such as relationships with other woman. Perhaps women understand each other better; deep, deep down, all of us feel a little temptation, or fantasize, about being with another woman. I am not a lesbian, I have never had sex with another woman, but after my problems, I lost interest in men. When I watch a romantic film and see two women kissing each other, I feel as if I could fall into the temptation of being with a female some day. I consider homosexuality normal and think that we have to take part in everything that nature asks in this world.

In the upper classes, although men and women do not have the financial problems as in the other social classes, many get married and then divorce each other shortly afterward fairly easily because the economic power is in their favor. Although there is also domestic violence, they just pay others to do it for them. There are people who accept any amount of money to beat, sexually abuse, or kill someone, as if it were nothing, and in this country there have been many cases of husbands or wives who contract these kind of people to kill their partners. Mostly they become suspects and are found guilty, but they often walk away free, as if it nothing had happened, due to the power of money or the influence they have. To give an example, a very famous man separated from his wife and she was murdered in her own home, together with her lover. On the day of the crime he even drove his car through the city with the police following him, as if he were the president and was being protected by the authorities. But this is not what happened, this man was running away from the crime he had committed. The case lasted a few months in court, but this man was ruled not guilty, a typical example of what happens with upper class people.

Chapter 15

DEATH SILENCES
DOMESTIC VIOLENCE

Here I have transcribed some comments by people from different parts of the world about domestic violence in Africa. I think it is interesting to see the point of view of people from different countries about violence against women in Africa.

Africa

A reporter from the University of Cape Town in South Africa said that four women are murdered by their partner in that country every day. He asked some questions to African women: When your partner insults you physically, emotionally, or sexually, do you report it or hide it? Should domestic violence be a private matter or should it be publicized? The vast majority of the women answered that this is normal, and that it is the way men have of showing how much they love them.

In Ethiopia, a man said that if he was married, his wife should not be able to take him to court for raping her, because only in cases of ill health can the wife deny her husband sex. He also said that if a wife does not want to have sex with her husband then she should divorce him, better that than accusing him of being a rapist.

In Guinea Bissau, the authorities do not care about domestic violence, and women are afraid of making any kind of comment. In one case, a man was sexually abused his thirteen-year-old stepdaughter and got her pregnant; the mother did not want to report him out of fear of losing her husband. Although women are more courageous about ending a relationship, in Africa many of them cannot make that decision because they are financially dependent on the men, especially when there are children involved.

Domestic violence is the silent death that destroys many lives. In Ghana, domestic violence seems to be allowed; men are the causes of so much abuse against women, and some of them suffer the worst violations. The rights of children, especially girls, are ignored, especially the right to education. They are left to go hungry, have nowhere to sleep, and are physically and psychologically tortured. The boys see what their parents are doing and often grow up to be violent men.

In Tomale, Ghana, some women are considered the property of their husbands, because their parents receive money from the respective husbands. It is normal in many parts of Africa to see a girl of fifteen marry an old man of seventy. In Ghana, a boy of six watched his father physically abuse his mother and was terrified because he thought his mother was going to die. How can this be love? How can one be in love and at the same time abuse the beloved? If this is love, no one should fall in love. In Ghana, they say that domestic violence should not be tolerated by anyone because it leads to separation; often mothers are the biggest victims.

Men from Ghana were asked who they would choose between their mothers or their fathers, seven out of ten men never hesitate in choosing their mothers, because of the impact they have had on their lives. But when you ask for their reaction when asking the same number of men if their daughters or sisters were severely beaten or sexually abused, they immediately respond that they would kill the abusers. But they forget that the women they choose as wives or girlfriends and whom they violate are also somebody's sisters and daughters.

A man has the right to physically mistreat his wife, but if he attacks another man in the street he will be arrested. He always argues that the tradition in Africa is for the woman to be subservient, which is convenient for him. The best advice given was that women should aim to get a good education and work hard to be independent, because when a woman is not completely dependent on a man, he will think twice before raising a finger against her.

In Kenya, domestic violence cannot be fought against, but the victims should be given some help, such as taking their cases to court or providing work. One woman experienced domestic violence for five years, and she hid it from everybody, even her best friend, thinking that one day this nightmare would end, but this was not so, and in the end, it all showed on her face.

In Sierra Leone, West Africa, some men abuse their wives using a kind of discipline, and we all know that these types of abuses are not socially accepted in other countries. The government should pass a strict law to educate these men. The women should also be educated about sex, because 99 percent of them do not know when they have been raped. There should be better education and laws against sexual, physical, and emotional violence.

In Lagos, Nigeria, they say that any man who feels a lot of energy should use it to put food on the table, because beating a woman is a sign of weakness. There, the women prefer to have a black eye or two than to get divorced, which is unbelievable. When the wives decide to report their husbands' violence, they are mostly arrested for being irresponsible, but they say that nothing positive will be done for them. Some of these married women cry more because of the abuses than about being mistreated, and in some cases, they end up being murdered when they are suspected of cheating on their husbands with a secret lover. These women never think of losing their husbands to other women.

In Malawi, some women say that they do not have any problem with a man who abuses them physically; they also accept that their husbands force them to have sex, for them this is part of being married.

In Senegal, one man said that many husbands continue to physically abuse their wives, and in many cases, they leave their bodies deformed from so many injuries.

In Sudan, there are tribes where it is normal for the man to show his love by beating his wife. In other areas of the country, it is generally claimed that sexual, physical, and emotional abuses should not be accepted. The problem with the Africans is that they do not even know that is physical violence is an act of abuse. Anyone who is abused by their husband or wife should report it to the police; the problem is that some policemen in Africa are the worst abusers, because they beat their own wives.

In Uganda, they say that a relationship should be based on mutual understanding, respect, and love, because no one deserves to suffer abuse and those that use domestic violence should be punished. There, they say that the first time a man beats a woman, it is only the beginning; if you cannot report it, let it be, because a person who loves somebody does not want to see their loved one crying. Likewise, when parents use violence to punish their children, afterward they treat them well. So, they are sure that domestic violence is a kind of rebellion, and once it starts, it does not stop.

In Zimbabwe, they say that domestic violence is very common.

United States of America

There is little help and little work for those women who accept and offer domestic advice out of fear of divorce because, when they get divorced, who will take care of her and of her children?

Much of this hatred of women is the result of the way men see women; this is cultural or even religious.

If men were the victims of domestic violence on a large scale, they would not resist having the addresses of their silent murderers published.

In New Jersey, one person suggested that African women should try to set up a type of union so that they can struggle against the silent death, and she also said that she was very surprised to find out that that the current vice president of the country was abused by her husband. This shows us how terrible Africa is in this area.

Domestic violence happens as part of a vicious circle that starts with words. After a short while, the guilty person is always remorseful and comes asking for forgiveness, and because the wife always loves the husband, when he asks for forgiveness they think that the violence is at an end, but this is not true. Throughout the world, domestic violence should be more openly commented on so that people can get the help they deserve.

Let us not forget that domestic violence does not exist just because a man beats a woman. There are women who are violent and abusive against their husbands and children. These are things that no one talks about, but everyone knows that this goes on. The men do not have the courage to say that their wives beat them or throw things at them, slap them, or spit on them. The abuses take different forms.

The abuses happen on both sides, for example, with boys who are sexually abused by maids, husbands who are mistreated on a daily basis by their wives, and they remain silent. People only see women as the victims.

Domestic violence is not only men's fault. In Africa they accept it when a man is physically or emotionally abusive of his wife. In Nigeria, a man who abuses his wife will be arrested, as a man who will have no public respect. Mostly in America, women mix up domestic violence with revenge by denouncing their husbands. In some cases, these allegations are turned into a weapon of control, of intimidation, and of economic exploitation of the man, and this has caused more violence against women. It is a big social problem, because there are more children growing up with only their mothers at home, without the presence of the father. This is the real tragedy.

In one situation, a wife took her husband to court in the United States for physical assault, and she was photographed to help her case, and the husband lost because of the evidence. The court said they knew the marks were caused by the husband, but he claimed she caused the marks on her own body in order to have him declared guilty.

It is very important for us to know that there is conflict between the heart (emotion) and the brain (reason), her head perhaps telling her to leave her abusive husband, but the heart says, I love him.

A man from Missouri said that domestic violence should not be dealt with in secret but rather in court.

England

From watching his mother being attacked, one man understood that it is wrong to treat a human being this way, and he felt great sympathy for all those who suffer in silence. He said there is help available, but it is the victim who has to help herself.

Japan

One person said that it was not a good idea to report domestic violence to the police in her country; even if the police take all the necessary steps, they end up saying that they are their lovers, if the women are not careful with what they say. She thinks that domestic violence does not exist. Why are so many of these things said by women?

Russia

It is said that it is horrible how many men treat their wives, and it does not matter how much he is offended, he should never lose control, nor his sense of humor, and he should find a friendly way to end things. For men who say that they love, ask them what they feel when the person they love is feeling pain?

Chapter 16

CASES OF PARENTS WHO PRACTICE DOMESTIC VIOLENCE AGAINST THEIR OWN CHILDREN

During my research I discovered that there are also cases of women who sacrifice their own children to be with the man they love. Some of them then take the lives they carried in their bellies for nine months to be with their men. It is hard for me to read about children who die at the hands of their parents as a result of domestic violence. Those who manage public or private organizations that provide services for children and adolescents can no longer allow their lives to be cut off at such a tender age. What can be done to avoid domestic violence, particularly against defenseless children, and stop it spreading in homes? When talking about children, we are also talking about our own children, and the pain a mother feels, we all feel. As for those who decide to end the lives of their own children, maybe there are problems that seem to have no solution, but if they find the help needed before a tragedy takes place, this could be avoided. Education and solidarity are two tools that could be used by society against domestic violence. The American government claims that the struggle lies in a basic reform of the law and shows that it begins, right there, with putting an end to ignorance. Many children die, and new laws are formed based on tragedies in the community. What I read in the newspaper or see on television is sad and painful, portraying so many children losing their lives.

United States of America

Arizona

In Phoenix, a woman who went to work every day usually left her one-year-old son with a babysitter. No one knows the reason why, but one day she left the child in her car. When she came out from work, seven hours later, the child was found dead in the car from the heat. She is in prison paying for her crime.

California

1. There was a woman who was separated and lived very comfortably with two children. Her ex-husband left her a very big and pretty house where she lived with her children. One night, she called 911, saying that someone had entered the house, taken a knife in the kitchen, gone up to the children's room, and stabbed them many, many times, killing them. Whilst the intruder was in the kitchen, she had heard one of the children who was still alive, dragging themselves across the floor, looking for help, but the intruder then took a knife once again and stabbed the child. It was then that the mother, who heard all this, went downstairs, and the intruder cut her arm and her neck. But the police were suspicious about her "story," because some weeks after the children had died, she was celebrating her birthday with many friends, fireworks, and cake. It seems she wanted to be absolutely free and the children were in her way. Everything she said about the intruder was made up, because she herself was the murderer.

2. A man, perhaps disoriented because his wife had died, did not know what to do, and as he was unable to take care of the child alone and wanted to distance himself from him, beat and killed the eighteen-month-old baby. He is in prison, paying for his crime.

3.   What is it that goes on in people's heads, especially mothers, for them to reach the point of doing what they do? In Tallman, one mother had the audacity to put her seven-year-old son in the oven; the poor child had burns over many parts of this his body. Why did she do that? Because the child had lost his cell phone. What kind of world are we in? The worst of it is that the child went to the nursery school and the teacher asked the child what had happened and who had done that to him, and he answered that his mother had put him in the oven. The woman called the mother to find out more and she denied it.

North Carolina

A policeman said that in thirteen years of service he had never seen such a horrible case as this one. When a mother got home, she found the head of her four-year-old daughter separated from her body and the person who committed this so brutal crime was none other than the father himself. He was captured and will pay for his crime.

Connecticut

One father brutally beat his son seven times for doing his school homework slowly and left him bleeding on the floor and went out. Thank God his sister called 911, reporting her own father for abusing her brother. The father was tried and found guilty and is paying for his crime.

Florida

A woman who had two children with a man from whom she was separated found a new love, who came to live with her and her children. One day an accident happened, or so the stepfather claimed. The seven-year-old boy was playing with a gun, and when he tried to take it off the child the gun went off, causing his death. But the boy's sister, who was there, told a different story. She said that she, her brother, her mother, and their stepfather were at home, and the brother started to cry, and the stepfather took the revolver and shot her brother in the face, in front of the mother, who did nothing to prevent it. The murderer tried to escape but was shot and killed by the police, and the mother was found guilty of not helping her own son. She is in prison, paying for her guilt.

Indiana

In Indianapolis, there was a student who was pregnant, and from what it seems, none of her classmates knew about it. On the day the child was born, she went to the bathroom, sat on the toilet seat, and gave birth. She let the baby die by drowning, and then she took the dead body and threw it in the trash. Someone found the body and called the authorities. She is in prison, paying for her crime.

Maryland

1. A woman seemed to be a mother of a normal family, bringing up her four children with her boyfriend. When the boyfriend arrived home, he found his girlfriend bleeding and took her to hospital. It was then discovered that she had given birth to a child and the police were called. She confessed that the child was born dead, that she had flushed the body down the toilet. The police did not believe her and went to her house to check it out. They found the body of the dead child under the sink, wrapped in a towel. Worst of all is that the bodies of another three children were found buried in the yard of the house. She is in prison, without right to bail, awaiting her trial to pay for her crimes.

2. In Salisbury, a man who lived with a daughter and his wife decided to kill the daughter for the millions of dollars in life insurance he had taken out if she were to die. The case was uncovered, and he is paying for his crime.

Missouri

This man was very tough and very controlling. He mistreated children and thought that everything should be done just as he wanted. For unknown reasons, he decided to kill his fourteen-year-old daughter, his son of eleven, another of eight years, and the smallest who was one year old, who is in hospital in a critical condition. The man was caught and is paying for his crimes.

New Jersey

1. A man lived for a long time with his girlfriend and her daughters. When she broke up with him he sought revenge and killed the two daughters, one of twenty and the other of fifteen; one of them was pregnant, and he killed himself.

2. A man was accused of sexually molesting two adolescents, one of them his girlfriend's daughter. As he was going to get over twenty years in jail, he also decided to kill his two children, one who was twelve and the other of eight, and then killed himself. What do the children have to do with their father's monstrosity? Who gave him the right to kill them?

3. This is one of many cases that have been happening because women have not yet got it into their heads that it is possible to go on with our children and our lives alone. If the men who father the children do not want to raise them, what makes women think that someone else will do? Many people invite men to live with them and their children after just a short time of dating, without knowing them properly. The woman in this case paid the very expensive price, and this will remain in her memory for ever. One woman was trying to make it alone with her newly born daughter without the father. She found a man who promised her all kinds of wonderful things, including looking after her daughter as if she were his own, and they started living together in her house. One day, she went out to work and left her three-month-old daughter with

her partner. When she returned, she found everything very quiet and started to call out to him. With no answer, she went to the room and found the bed covered in blood and no sign of him or of her daughter. Without losing any time, she called the police, who searched the whole house and found the child's dead body in a plastic bag. The poor child had been murdered by the monster, but thank God, he was caught and will pay for his crime.

4.   Another man committed the crime of killing his twelve-year-old son and his eight-year-old daughter; no one knows why.

5.   There was an unfortunate child who lived with his parents and had already suffered physical abuse by the time he was only two years old. After his parents separated and his mother found another husband, this stepfather shook the child so much and hit him with a hard object, that the poor thing went into a coma, with his face all deformed. His own mother was present and did nothing to stop the attack, and when help arrived, unfortunately the child was already dead. His organs were donated to save the lives of others, and the criminals were sentenced to pay for their crime.

New York

1.   This was another case that shook the whole world: a child lived with her mother and brothers and her perverse stepfather. He beat her, tied her up, made her eat cat food, and abused her sexually. Then he killed her. What kind of monster did this?

2.   A child of just ten witnessed her mother's boyfriend physically abuse her four-year-old brother. She testified against him and her mother. The girl said that this guy had mistreated her brother a lot; one day he even pushed him so that the television fell on top of him. He was knocked unconscious and stopped breathing; she called her mother's boyfriend, and he came and gave him mouth to mouth resuscitation and he recovered, but

then he took the child by the neck and started to beat him against the wall. The girl started to cry and begged him to stop hitting her brother. She anxiously waited for her mother to say something, thinking that she would do something, but she was disappointed because her mother did nothing. That same night, the brother was vomiting blood in the bathroom, and she asked both of them to take her brother to the doctor, but neither of them did anything and the poor child died. The man confessed to his guilt and will spend twenty-five years in prison. The child's mother was sentenced to four years in prison. Is that all?

3. Another man was divorced from his wife, and they were both getting on fine until one day his ex disappeared with their child. A few days later, the body of his child, who was just a few months old, was found. The saddest thing is that some toys were found nearby along with his diapers and feeding bottles. The father is paying for his crime.

4. A woman arrived at hospital to give birth to a child that had been conceived as the result of a rape. It was born premature, and it was kept there until it was out of danger and could be handed over to the mother. Once it was doing okay, the child was handed over to the mother, and they asked her to return in a few days, but she never went back to the hospital. This mother called 911, saying that someone had stolen her child. The police moved heaven and earth but found nothing, because the child had not been stolen, but rather had been murdered by her own hand. She covered the child's face with a sheet and then threw it in the trash. The excuse she gave was that she was married and had children with her husband and didn't want to have problems, because she knew her husband would not believe she had been raped. She is now in prison, paying for her crime.

5. There was a woman who worked as a babysitter in a family home, and she did her job very well, then one day left on her day off. Her employers were surprised later when they heard

that she was pregnant and had given birth in the bathroom of a bus station, put the child in a shoe box, and threw it in the trash. The excuse she gave was that she didn't want to bring up a child without a husband. Why did she have sex then? She should have kept her legs together or used a rubber! She was tried and found guilty and is paying for her crime.

6. A nine-year-old child begged his sick mother to get help. The next day, after her fiancé went out to work, the mother and son were talking about the dreams they had in front of the television. Out of the blue, she decided to hold the pillow over the face of her son until he stopped breathing, and then she went out and tried to throw herself under a train. When help came she was taken to hospital, suffering from depression and taking medication. If she is found guilty, she will get twenty-five years in jail. May God have pity on her.

7. A seven-year-old child had arrived dead at hospital and they said he had had an epileptic attack. The employees suspected that he had died of a heart attack. The child had a long suffering history with bad parents. In 2001, he had been handed over to the father, and in 2003, he suffered a leg fracture and another to his spine. His father said that they had been playing, but what kind of game is this for a child to be hurt like this? Worst of all, in the same year, he had kicked him in his stomach and had not called 911. When he did decide to call, two days later, he was already dead. He is in prison paying for his crime. The death of this child could have been avoided if the authorities had taken him away.

8. Another dead child in New York. The police could find no sign of trauma on the child's body and did not know what had caused its death. A neighbor who went to visit her friend saw the child lying face down on its bed, at about two in the afternoon. The child's face, legs, and arms were cold and its body laid out, and so she turned to her friend and asked what had happened to the child, but it was already dead. Worst of all is that there had already been a summons against her for

abuse. She also had a history of drug use and is undergoing treatment. How can children be left in the hands of these people with so many problems? This case could also have been avoided if the law were stricter.

9.   Yet more cases of children being abused by their parents include two of the most infamous cases of child abuse in the city's history. One of these children was a six-year-old beautiful girl. It is very painful to have to write about this case, but it is necessary so that everyone can hear the facts. In 1995, this child was left hungry, maltreated physically, and murdered by her own mother. A few years afterward, another child of seven was also murdered almost exactly the same way. The stepfather was found guilty of her death. He said she had been disobedient and needed to be disciplined. She was held prisoner in her own room, tied to a chair, and forced to use a cat litter tray as her bathroom, according to the authorities. Perhaps these deaths could have been avoided if the city agency that looks after the custody of abused children had acted differently. City officials had been warned five times that this six-year-old child was being abused. This child asked for help when she complained to the social worker that her mother had been slapping her. The mother of this child also commented to the social worker that her daughter had defecated in the bed and had put feces in the refrigerator, which would be very strange if it were true. In the case of the other girl, why had they not investigated when she was absent from school and had been given no explanation? The second time, a teacher realized that she had injuries on her head suggestive of violence. A period of sixty days was given for the investigation of complaints, but no action was taken in time to save the children.

10. A girl of thirteen gave birth to a baby and afterward threw him out of the window of her bedroom. When her boyfriend got home to the apartment to visit her and she told him what she had done, they went down, rolled up the body in a towel, and took it to hospital, but on the way they started to feel

afraid and put the baby's body in a bag and left it at the door of a church. The authorities found them guilty, and the two of them are paying for their crime.

11. A mother who had been declared mentally unstable said she was innocent of having slapped and kicked her three-year-old daughter to death. People told the authorities that it was common for the mother to beat her child when she was angry. Worst of all, she is pregnant with another child. How can they let this happen if they know she has a mental problem? Why didn't they do anything so that she did not give birth again?

12. A child was born with cocaine in its bloodstream and was adopted by a family who went on to see it crawling, walking, and saying its first words. The adoptive father said he had brought her up and treated her like she were his own daughter, but the biological father beat her so much that at the age of seven, he killed her. The real father asked for forgiveness, saying that it was an accident, but the authorities said otherwise, because this was not the only time he had done this. These people have to pay for their crimes. He was sentenced to spend a very long time in prison.

13. In 2003, a child who was just two years died, and in 2005, another four children died at the hands of their parents, one aged sixteen months, was drowned, another who was one year old was beaten to death, and another of five died in a fire that was set alight in the house, and one of seven was beaten by the father for two days until he died. In 2006, a child of two months was shaken by the father and died, and another who was five months old was drowned. Another one who was two years old died of a blow to the head, and another who was four died from the injuries he had received, and another who was four was tortured, beaten various times, and then killed. As everyone can see, all these defenseless children were mistreated and murdered by the people who brought them into the world, the first people they saw when they opened their eyes for the first time, the people who are obliged to

protect them and be responsible for them, give them love and care as they raise them, as their parents had done with them.

14. In Coney Island, a man had lived for many years with his companion, who had a daughter of seven. Because they couldn't get along, they separated and each went their own way. But he was unable to accept losing her and was very jealous when he saw her with another. When his daughter went to visit him in his apartment, he called his ex a few hours later, telling her what he was planning to do. In despair, she called 911, but when the police arrived, it was already too late, and they found the daughter's body along with that of the father. No one, not the family, neighbors, or friends, could believe he was capable of killing his daughter, who he adored so much, and taking his own life.

Ohio

This other case made me ill, I don't know what to call a person who puts their own child in a microwave oven. What does a monster like this deserve? This woman took her daughter who was just a few months old and put her in the microwave; she suffered many burns and died in hospital.

Texas

1. A woman had three children, two with her husband and another she had from a fling she had while still married. This very good man recognized the child as his own and everyone adored him. After a few years, things were not going so well, they separated, and he started a new relationship with someone from work. She also remarried, but she remained crazy about him, and she was very jealous of his relationship with his new wife and wanted him to live with her. But there was one big problem: the children. She didn't want to take care of or bring up her children. The only solution she found

was to take the three children in the car, then she took out her revolver and shot them. The bullets left the smallest paralyzed in a wheelchair, the first one paralyzed on one side and with no voice, but unfortunately the third one died. The mother's story was that she had been assaulted by thieves trying to steal her car and they had shot her children, but she was only shot in the arm. All this for a man like that. Thanks to the daughter who recovered and could tell the police that her own mother had murdered her sister and tried to kill her and her brother, she was given a life sentence.

2. A man argued with his girlfriend and ended up killing her seven-year-old son and his own unborn son, who was due to be born two months later. May God care for our children, releasing them from the hands of these perverted people.

3. There is yet another case of a woman who had depression and killed her five children.

Virginia

1. Another case involved a mother who put her one-month-old son in the microwave oven. She said she doesn't remember having put her son in the microwave and switched it on until he was cremated. My God, what a tragedy.

2. A mother made her child sick whilst he was just a few days old. He was taken to hospital ten times, she injected so much insulin into the child that he was paralyzed, was unable to walk, and was fed by tubes. He died afterward. She is paying for her crime.

3. A father went to visit his two children, who were studying at university. No one realized what this man was about to do as everything seemed so normal. When the three had met, for no reason, the father took out a gun and killed his two

children, and then he killed himself. May God forgive this man's soul.

West Virginia

1. In North Charleston, more children paid for their parents' domestic violence. Four children were murdered by their own father in this city.

2. Also in North Charleston, a man wanted to take revenge by taking the lives of his four children. The bodies were found in the house by a neighbor who called the authorities. When they arrived, they found the father trying to escape, but he was caught and will pay for his crimes.

Washington

1. A divorced man was given custody of his two children and was starting a new family. For financial reasons, the man killed his son, after he had put his boy's name on a life insurance policy for thousands of dollars. What use will this money be to him, now he will be in prison for many years?

2. No one knows how the children's protectors let it happen, because this mother must be crazy. The decomposed bodies of her daughters of five and sixteen years were found in her house, and she is being charged with the crimes.

Other Countries

Belgium

No one knows why this mother committed this barbarity. One morning she sent her five children to school and that afternoon she was waiting for them, with a dagger, and she killed them one by one. She only left a simple note to a friend saying she could not take any more. This was the only solution she found to get rid of the children. Who is she to make such a decision?

Brazil

A married woman had two children. From the video that was shown on the TV, it seemed that they were very happy. She liked to go out alone to have fun with friends, leaving the children uncared for. Then her husband decided to ask for a divorce, and she was given custody of the children. After a few months, she found a new partner and thought it would last forever. That was until she invited him to live with her, but he was not ready, and so she was left without a husband and without children, because she killed them all.

Peru

1. A man became upset with his son when he lost a neighbor's cell phone. He took his child's hands and put them in the fire. The burns were so severe that the child couldn't touch anything. I don't know why they do these things and then don't want to pay for the consequences. He left the child inside the house without medical care so he would not be reported, but he was charged, tried, and is in prison for his crime.

2. In Lima, a married woman lived with her mother and brothers, and she got pregnant. When her husband found out that she was pregnant, he asked her to have an abortion, but she refused and had the child. As always, when she went out to work, she left her husband looking after the child, as he had no job. Her mother had already warned her that she had seen the guy beating up her younger brothers, but she didn't think he would go so far. When the grandmother got home from work, she found one of her children outside, saying that her grandson was dead. She ran into the room and found the

naked body of her grandson, and she asked the father what had happened. He said that the eight-month-old child had fallen out of bed. The grandmother took the child to hospital along with the father, and they wanted to arrest her right there as they saw that the child had suffered physical violence. She then explained to them that she had nothing to do with what was going on and that the father had been taking care of the child. He confessed that he had punched the child and had left his body covered in blood and that he had hidden the blood covered clothes under the mattress. He was arrested at the hospital and is paying for his crime. But do you think the story was over? Even with the husband's statement, the wife did not believe he had killed her son, she feels so sorry for him that she always goes to the prison to visit her dear husband, and she is now pregnant again by her own son's murderer. But she said that his family is threatening her, her mother and her small brothers, saying that they will kill them one by one. With all the threats, she shouldn't be with him at all, much less get pregnant by her own son's murderer. This creature needs psychiatric help.

3. A man brutally beat his son, leaving him unconscious, and why? Because the child wet the bed. When he saw that the child hadn't woken up, he threw kerosene on the child's body and set him on fire. He buried the remains of his son in the yard but was found out, because the neighbor's dog was eating the child's foot. What cruelty! The murderer was arrested to pay for his crime.

Puerto Rico

This other case also happened with a man who, jealous of his wife, killed one of his wife's daughters and then escaped, upset that he hadn't killed all of them. What do the children have to do with this, to pay such a high price? He was arrested.

Dominican Republic

1.   In Santo Domingo, the largest city in this country, a single man had a woman who took care of his daughters, and they seemed to like each other. His fiancé found out about this, and burning with jealousy, she waited until everyone was sleep and came in armed with a big knife and brutally killed the two innocent children, leaving their bodies unrecognizable. She said she thought she was killing the father, not the children.

2.   Also in Santo Domingo, a woman lived with her boyfriend and a three-year-old daughter from her previous partner. The neighbors had already seen that both the stepfather and the mother herself physically abused the child. One of the neighbors had even called the authorities, but no action was taken. It was not long before something awful happened. One day, the mother went out to work and left her boyfriend taking care of the child. Furious at being woken up by child's crying, he took a broom and hit the child so much that she fell unconscious with fractured bones. The doctors do not know whether he penetrated the child or if he used the broomstick on her, because she was penetrated so brutally that some organs were destroyed, killing her. He was caught in the hospital itself, where he had taken the child, saying she had fallen out of bed. The hospital employees didn't believe him and called the police. His girlfriend will also pay for this brutal crime.

Chapter 17

CASES OF CHILDREN WHO MURDER THEIR PARENTS AND SIBLINGS

Violence has generally increased throughout the world, as well as crimes committed by young people and adolescents, who often are children that live or have lived with domestic violence. These cases were also transcribed from the media because they caught my attention.

United States of America

California

1. This case happened with a very well-to-do family who had one son and one daughter. The father, the mother, and the daughter returned from vacation and were happy to see the son well; he also seemed content and everything returned to normal. One day the husband went to work, and the mother and daughter went out together. The son contracted a friend from college to kill the family; he gave him the key to the house and told him where to find the bullets in his parents' room. They prepared everything, and the friend went inside the house and waited for the family. When the sister came in, he shot her; when the mother came in, she saw her daughter's body and ran out, but the friend ran after her and shot her several times too, and then he waited in the house for a few hours, waiting for the father. When he heard the

man open the door, he shot him many times in the doorway, and he fell down dead. Then the youth disappeared. After the investigation, the son confessed that he had asked his friend to murder his family because he didn't want to share the money with his sister and didn't want to wait for his parents to die of natural causes because that would take too long. Both of them were convicted and are paying for their crimes.

2. In Hollywood, a couple had two children, who they gave the best of everything, sending them to the best schools. They grew up with the father always telling them to be good men. One day the young men decided to kill their own parents and bought a revolver. They waited for them to fall asleep on the couch and shot the father and the mother many times, leaving them dead. They went out and got rid of the gun, returned home, and called 911, saying that when they came home, they found their parents dead. Everyone was shocked at these events, and it seemed the case was closed. They got on with their lives, spending a lot of money, buying a new apartment and cars, living the life they had always wanted, until the youngest son began to feel remorse for what they had done and told his psychologist. Everything was found out. They confessed, saying that their father had abused one of them sexually and that the mother knew and did nothing to stop the sexual violence. They were convicted and are paying for their crimes.

Illinois

In Chicago, a man had a very good job and was respected. He had married for the second time and was living with his new wife, two small daughters, and the oldest son from his first marriage. As far as everyone was concerned, everything seemed to be fine, but his son thought differently, and he thought that his father and his stepmother preferred the two other children, and so he decided to take justice into his own hands. One day he arranged for his friends to go into the house and murder the whole family, which they did. He waited for them all to sleep, opened the door for his friends to come in, and all together, sub-machine gun in hand, they killed the two children, the mother, and the father. He told the police that thieves had broken into the house to steal things and had killed his whole family. But after much investigation, it was discovered that he and his friends were the guilty parties, and they received their punishment.

Maryland

This very sad case took place in Baltimore, involving a boy of just fifteen years of age. His friends said that he was always complaining, saying he had a problem with his father, but they hadn't thought it was that serious. One day, he waited for everyone in the family to fall asleep, took his father's revolver, and killed his family. When the police got to the house they found the father's body covered in blood in the bedroom along with that of his mother and his two brothers, one who was thirteen years old and the other eleven. After he had killed his family, he went out but then returned later on. After a few hours, he called the police, saying he had found his father dead in the house. He was arrested, and the case was so serious that the death penalty was called for, but because he is a child, the law will not allow him to be executed. May God forgive him for all these crimes he committed.

New York

1. A poor family lived in a building, and the mother was a militant woman who brought up her children alone. Everyone admired her for this. But everything changed from one day to the next when the police went to the barbershop where her eldest son worked, asking his work colleagues questions about him. They said that he had a problem at home with the family, but they didn't think he would kill his mother and brother in the apartment. He then cut up their bodies into pieces, put them into plastic bags, and threw them into the river. The neighbors couldn't believe this had happened.

2. A mother said she didn't care what her son did, she would never stop wanting the best for him, because he was a present from God. Even after, in his mother' own house and in front of her small son, he took out a revolver and shot his father and brother in the back. He was tried and sentenced to many, many years in prison.

3. A woman had five children, the eldest from another man, the other four with her fiancé. He was a man who took drugs and was always physically abusive when he wanted money for his addiction. One day, he came home drunk and started to argue and beat up his wife. The oldest son couldn't take any more abuse; he picked up a pair of scissors and stabbed the stepfather many times until he was dead. I feel very sorry for this boy, a quiet, intelligent boy, a good student at school, but he is in prison, paying for his crime. This kind of crime is hard on everyone, especially for the sixteen-year-old boy who had his whole life ahead of him, loved by everyone, a child who could no longer take his mother being mistreated and being crushed by her companion. May God take care of this child, and may he receive the help he needs.

4. A twenty-two-year-old woman had a small daughter of two years, but one day she and some friends committed a robbery, and she was imprisoned; custody of her daughter was given to her mother. She was imprisoned for seventy-eight days, and when she was released, a fight started because she wanted her daughter back. Because of this argument, she picked up a knife and stabbed her forty-seven-year-old mother to death. The noise woke up her daughter, as well as her fourteen-year-old brother. When he saw the mother bleeding, he called 911. After the young woman had murdered her own mother, she left the house but was caught a few hours later. She will pay for her crime. Who could be a better mother than the grandmother who had already been a mother?

5. In Long Island, a twenty-year-old lad lived with his mother and stepfather. He waited until the stepfather was sleeping

and killed him, beating him to death. He said the stepfather was molesting him sexually and that he physically abused his mother, but people also say that it was really because of the life insurance for a few million dollars. A friend of his helped him hide the evidence of the crime. He also said he had not murdered his stepfather and that it had been his own mother, which the police believe is impossible. He was sentenced to twenty-five years in prison.

6.   In Staten Island, a twenty-six-year-old woman had been sexually molested by her father when she was two. Now an adult, she decided to take justice into her own hands and murdered her own father. She said that she was sexually abused not only by him but also by others in the family and that everyone knew about it and did nothing to stop it. She is suffering from depression and is being monitored in the Staten Island Psychiatric Ward.

7.   In Westchester, a daughter killed her own mother, stabbing her to death for unknown reasons. Everyone in the family said she was a good daughter, but none of them knew what happened for her to act this way. The jury only took four hours to send her to prison for twenty-five years.

Pennsylvania

A fourteen-year-old girl was going out with a lad of eighteen. He said that when he couldn't reach her on the phone, he decided to go to her house, but he didn't find her because the father had prohibited her from continuing that relationship. So he decided to kill his girlfriend's father and mother, and then he took their car and left. Later, he decided to return, not caring whether he was caught by the police, and he saw his girlfriend; he stopped and she got in the car and they made their escape. When the police found them, they were already in Indianapolis. He said they were hoping to build a new life together. They decided that she was his captive. He is now in prison for his crime.

Chapter 18

LOVE INSIDE AND OUTSIDE OF PRISON

There are many cases of women who have relationships with the most dangerous criminals in prison, and usually they end up getting married to them and starting a family.

What I am going to discuss in this chapter is impressive; I had to see it with my own eyes to believe it, and I will continue to search out the most brutal cases so that everyone can become aware of how a home, which should be a peaceful place, full of tranquility and happiness, can become distorted. I hope that these cases make a difference in many homes. After everything I have researched, I ended up believing that there are not many normal people out there in the world. It is the eternal debate between what the essence of man is and what is cultural, acquired from the environment they live in.

I have a twenty-two-year-old son, and whenever I am at home in the afternoon I read the newspaper and watch the news on television, and he always asks me why. One day I started to explain to him about domestic violence. And then he started to help me, and whenever he saw any news about domestic violence, he would take notes and give them to me to write about in my book.

These cases come from a maximum security prison, which is where murderers are held. I still cannot believe why some men and women who live normal lives have a fascination for this kind of person. How does the family of the victims feel when they see someone with a criminal record sending and receiving e-mail?

1. A man killed his pregnant wife and received thousands of letters in prison.

2. Two brothers murdered their parents whilst they were sleeping, sat on the couch, and even received marriage proposals from women who lived a normal life and never committed any kind of crime.

3. A young seventeen-year-old girl killed her mother because she didn't like her boyfriend. She received e-mails from many men outside of prison.

4. A man who killed another man for no reason also received letters from women outside of prison.

5. A woman who robbed a small store and stabbed an elderly man to death also received e-mails from men who live normal lives.

6. Another man who beat his teacher to death communicates via the Internet from inside prison with women who have normal lives.

7. In Los Angeles, a man who killed more than ten women, whom he tortured, sexually assaulted, and then strangled, received a visit from a woman who was curious to meet him. When she got to the prison, she said she felt nothing for him, but they talked and he even managed to get her phone number. After a few days, she received the first call from him in prison, and as time passed, she started to like him. One thing led to another, and he started to control and to manipulate her. As she fell for his game, from inside the prison he planned to murder this woman in the same way he had killed the others, so they would think that the murderer was free and that he was innocent.

I cannot understand how he convinced her in this way, or how she let herself be convinced, but the fact is that she fell for his game, and he tried to murder her. The end of the story was that he failed and was sentenced to attempted murder. The person who was free lost everything and everyone. I ask myself if this is normal.

8. There was another woman who put her two children in the car and pushed it into the river, killing them because her boyfriend didn't like children. She received ten thousand letters from admirers.

9. For a bank robber who was interviewed by a journalist, it was love at first sight, and he started to call her every day, and she even paid his bail and he left prison. They were married and he started stealing again and was sent back to prison.

10. A molester received a visitor who fell in love with him, and they were married in prison.

11. A woman who was imprisoned for murder kept sending letters to men outside of jail. A man who started answering the letters fell desperately in love with her and decided to marry her. They were married in prison, she became pregnant, and they had a daughter. Her husband and his mother took care of the child. After twenty-three years in prison, she is now a free woman and has a new life with her husband, her daughter, and also her mother-in-law, as a united family.

12. A murderer fell in love with a woman who had her own life on the outside. She had been married before and had separated from her husband, leaving her with two children. After a few years, she had a boyfriend who helped her take care of her children. Through bad luck, one day her friend asked her to accompany her on a visit to her lover who was in prison, and she accepted, and when they arrived there, she met another prisoner and fell in love with him. They are now married, although he is still in prison.

I still cannot understand why all this happens and ask myself what kind of world we are living in! Why do we hate each other so much? Why can't we love each other enough to give our children a better life? Why don't we try to explain that this life we are leading is not the true one? Why don't we try to talk to them and tell them there is true love, without any kind of violence, and that we want a better relationship for them than ours?

We should do a bit of everything; we should always try to inform and educate, so people know what kind of world we are living in. Nowadays I think completely differently; I don't trust people like before. And it is hard because we can't see what each person is thinking, what that person could do. It is hard to see a man and a woman swear eternal love and then kill each other or kill their children.

Many people do not know about these cases because they do not watch the news on television, read newspapers, or talk to other people. There is also a serious aggravating fact in all this and that's misinformation. Most cases of domestic violence are not reported, and when they are, they are not publicized—they merely become police statistics.

DOMESTIC VIOLENCE RESOURCES

Here are some organizations that offer assistance to the victims of domestic violence:

Brazil

(Data supplied by Marta Leiro, from the Bahia Women's Forum)

Women's Call Line, or call 180, works twenty-four hours a day; the call is free and can be made from anywhere in Brazil.

The call center works with operators who are trained in matters of gender, on federal government policies for women, guidance on dealing with violence against women, and especially on how to receive a report and to take in the women. They use a database with more than 260 questions and answers developed based on information available at the Secretariat of Special Policies for Women (SPM) and on all the reports already received by our Ombudsman.

According to SPM, the Call 180 service has 50 attendance points and has been using Direct Call Transfer VOIP technology since 2009, which allows the data from the calls received to be systematized automatically (date, place of origin, time, and call duration). www.agenciapatriciagalvao.org.br/index.php?option=com_content&view=article&lid=189:como-funciona-o-ligue-180-a-central-de-atendimento-a-woman&catid=51 :pautas

Bahia

Special Attention to Woman Police Station
Salvador, BA
Tel.: (71) 3247-0205 / 3245-5481
CREAIDS: State AIDS Reference Center
Salvador, BA
Tel.: (71) 3382-5737 / 3328-0992 / 3328-0552 creaids@creaids.gov.
ba.br

IPERBA: Bahia Perinatology Institute
Salvador, BA
Tel.: (71) 3453-6400 / 3453-6409 / 3453-6404

IMLNR; Nina Rodrigues Legal Medicine Institute
Salvador, BA
Tel.: (71) 3116-8600

Public Defender Legal Assistance
Salvador, BA
Tel.: (71) 3336-5507

SPM: Special Policies for Women Superintendency
Salvador, BA
Tel.: (71) 3321-3494 / 3321-3817 sepm@salvador.ba.gov.br

Calafate Women's Collective
Salvador, BA
Tel.: (71) 3258-0911 coletivodemulheresdocalafate@uol.com.br or
cmcssa@ibest.com.br

CHAME: Women's Humanitarian Support Center
Salvador, BA
Tel.: (71) 3321-9166 / 3321-9100 ong@chame.org.br www.chame.
org.br

Loreta Valadares Reference Center: Prevention and Attention to
  Women in Situations of Violence
Tel.: (71) 3235 4268

Live Project/IMLNR: Attention to Persons in Situation of Sexual
  Violence Services
Salvador, BA
Tel.: (71) 3117-6700 / 3117-6702

United States of America

National Domestic Violence Hotline, a free number that deals with the
highest number of people seeking assistance as victims of abuse. Their
web site is www.ndvh.org. For assistance call (800) 799-7233 or (800)
787-3224.

Alabama

Alabama Coalition Against Domestic Violence
P. O. Box 4762
Montgomery, Alabama 36101
Telephone (334) 832-4842, (800) 650-6522
Fax (334) 832-4803 http://www.acadv.org

California

California Alliance Against Domestic Violence
9265 Street, Suite 1000
Sacramento, California 95814
Telephone (916) 444-7163, (800) 524-4765
Fax (916) 444-7165 http://www.caadv.org

Connecticut

Connecticut Coalition Against Domestic Violence
90 Pitkin Street
East Hartford, Connecticut 06108
Telephone (860) 282-7899, (888) 774-2900 info@actadv.org

Maryland

Maryland Network Against Domestic Violence
6911 Laurel-Bowie Road, Suite 309
Bowie, Maryland 20715
Telephone (301) 352-4547, (800) MD-HELPS
Fax (301) 809-0422 http://www.mnadv.org

Michigan

Michigan Coalition Against Domestic Violence
3893 Okemos Road, Suite B2
Okemos, Michigan 48864
Telephone (517) 347-7000
Fax (517) 347-8470
TTY (547) 381-8470 http://www.mcadsv.org

New Jersey

New Jersey Coalition for Women
1670 White Horse Hamilton Square Road
Trenton, New Jersey 08690
Telephone (609) 584-9750, (800) 572-7233, (800) 224-0211 (for
    lesbians)
Fax (609)584-9750
TTY (609) 584-9750 http://www.njcbw.org

New York

New York State Coalition Against Domestic Violence
79 Central Avenue
Albany, New York 12206
Telephone (518) 432-4867, (800) 942-6906, (800) 980-7660
    (Spanish)
Fax (518) 463-3155

Texas

Texas Council for the Family in Violence
8701 P. O. Box 161810
Austin, Texas 78716
Telephone (512) 794-1133
Fax (512) 794-1199 http://www.tefw.org

Puerto Rico

Puerto Rico Peace for Women (Includes Coalition Against
    Domestic Violence Project)
P. O. Box 1007
RMS 108
San Juan, Puerto Rico 00919
Telephone (487) 281-7579
Fax (787) 767-6843
Pazparalamujer@yunque.net

GLOSSARY

Bodily injury: concerns aggression that offends one's bodily integrity or health.

Discrimination against women: every distinction, exclusion, or restriction based on sex and which has the objective or result of prejudicing or preventing recognition, enjoyment, or exercising of human rights and fundamental freedoms by women in political, economic, social, cultural, and civil areas, or in any other area.

Domestic violence: violence that takes place in the home, in the domestic environment, or in a family.

Family violence: violence that takes place within the family, that is, in the relationships between the members of a family community, formed by natural family ties (father, mother, daughter, etc.), by civil ties (husband, mother-in-law, stepfather, etc.), by affinity (cousin or uncle), or by affectivity (friend who lives in the same house).

Gender violence: violence suffered by women, without the distinctions of race, social class, religion, age, or any other condition, which is a product of the social system that subordinates the female sex.

Incestuous rape: rape practiced by a relation with hierarchic authority over the victim.

Institutional violence: type of violence motivated by inequality (gender, ethnic, racial, economic, etc.) predominant in different societies. These inequalities are formalized and institutionalized in the various private and state organizations, as well as in the different groups that make up these societies.

Interfamily violence: takes place in the home or domestic unit and generally is carried out by a member of the family who lives with the victim. Includes physical abuse, sexual abuse, psychological abuse, negligence, and abandonment.

Moral violence: action designed to cause calumny, defamation, or injury to someone's honor or reputation.

Physical violence: action that puts one's physical integrity at risk or causes physical damage.

Psychological violence: action designed to degrade or control the actions, behavior, beliefs, or decisions of another by means of intimidation, manipulation, direct or indirect threat, humiliation, isolation, or any other conduct that implies loss of psychological health, self-determination, or personal development.

Rape: violent copulation, without consent from one of the parties; forced coitus. May be carried out by just one person or by more than one individual (gang rape or gang bang).

Sexual abuse: involvement of children and adolescents in sexual activities, generally repetitive and intentional on the part of the abuser, that the victims do not completely understand and that violate the social and family rules of our culture.

Sexual assault: to oblige someone using violence or serious threat to practice acts of a sexual nature, in order to feel sexual pleasure.

Sexual exploitation: refers to the business of sexual relationships. The sexual exploitation of children and adolescents is a commercialized relationship of power and sexuality that aims to obtain advantages for adults and which causes biological/psychological/social damage to those exploited.

Sexual harassment in the work place: consists of asking for sexual favors by means of acts or verbal, nonverbal, or physical conduct based on asymmetric power relationships between the person instigating it and the victim, creating a hostile, abusive, and offensive work environment.

Sexual violence: an action that obliges a person to maintain sexual, physical, or verbal contact or to participate in other sexual relationships using force, intimidation, coercion, blackmail, bribery, manipulation, threat, or any other mechanism that limits personal free will. The aggressor obliging the victim to perform such acts with third parties is also considered sexual violence. According to the Brazilian Criminal Code, sexual violence may be characterized as physical or psychological or with the use of threats, including rape, attempted rape, seduction, or sexual assault.

Special Criminal Court: A small claims court set up for the conciliation, process, judgment, and execution of cases within its power, with the process driven by the criteria of speaking and maintaining simplicity, informality, procedural economy, and speed, always seeking conciliation or transaction as far as possible.

Specialized Attendance of Women Police Stations (DEAM): These police stations were set up to attend to women who are victims of violence or other crimes provided for in the Criminal Code. These police stations, also called Women's Police Stations (DDM), provide guidance for women on their rights, record complaints, open police inquiries, make arrests, and can refer them for physical examinations. After registering an incident, a police inquiry may be set up. The investigation listens to the victim and people involved in the case, that is, the aggressor and witnesses. Most of the cases that are dealt with are for threats and physical aggression.

Threat: action of intimidation, through words, writing, or gesture, or any other symbolic means, of promising to cause someone harm.

Trafficking of women: trafficking of women involves the recruitment and transit to work or jobs, within or beyond national borders, by means of violence or threat of violence, abuse of authority or dominant position, captivity through debt, fraud, and other forms of coercion. (See section below.)

Violence: an (inadequate) form of resolving conflict, representing an abuse of power. It is the law of the strongest over the weakest. Its consequences are heightened fear, insecurity, and revulsion, leading to low self-esteem and productive capacity; depression and isolation; and diminishment of defense systems, generating psychosomatic diseases.

Violence against women: any conduct or act of discrimination, aggression, or coercion caused by the simple fact of the victim being a woman and that causes damage, death, embarrassment, limitation, or physical, sexual, moral, psychological, social, political, or economic suffering, as well as loss of property. This violence may take place in public or private. (See section below.)

Violence to property: act of violence that implies damage, loss, removal, or destruction of objects, personal documents, goods, and values.

What Is Violence against Women?

In the definition of the Convention of Belem, Para (Inter-American Convention to Prevent, Punish and Eradicate Violence Against Women, adopted by OAS in 1994), violence against women is "any act or conduct, based on gender, which causes death or physical, sexual, or psychological harm or suffering to women, whether in the public or the private sphere." Violence against women is a manifestation of the historically unequal power relations between women and men that lead to the domination and discrimination against women by men and which impedes the full progress of women."

The United Nations Conference on Human Rights (Vienna, 1993) formally recognized violence against women as a violation of human rights.

Since then, the governments of the member countries of the UN and nonprofit organizations have worked toward eliminating of this kind of violence, which is also recognized as a serious public health problem. According to the World Health Organization, "the consequences of abuse are deep, going beyond the health and individual happiness and affecting the well-being of entire communities."

Where Does Violence against Women Come From?

It happens because in our society, many people still think that the best way of resolving conflict is through violence, and that men are stronger than and superior to women. And so often, husbands, boyfriends, parents, brothers, bosses, and other men think they have the right to impose their will on women. Although often alcohol, illegal drugs, and jealousy are indicated as factors that result in violence against women, at its root is the way in which society places greater value on men, which in turn is reflected in the way boys and girls are educated. Whereas boys are encouraged to value aggression, physical strength, action, domination, and satisfying their desires, including sexual ones, girls are valued for their beauty, gentleness, seduction, submission, dependency, sentimentalism, passivity, and care for others.

Violence and Religion

Violence against women is a very old phenomenon and is seen as the most practiced hidden crime in the world.

It has been legalized over the ages by religious and secular laws, legitimized by different cultures and by myths of the oral or written tradition.

In the course of the relationship between violence and religion, the group Catholics For the Right to Decide said, "The legitimacy that religion has given to the subordination of woman is not in its essence divine."

We have the right to question and challenge theological and religious teachings that encourage the authority of man and the subordination of women, thus sustaining violence.

One must suspect the sacred images that may be legitimizing violent relationships and that are motivating the eternal discrimination and inequality between men and women.

Violence and Health (Physical and Psychological)

Violence against women, as well as being a political, cultural, police, and legal question, is principally a question of public health. Many women become ill because of situations of violence at home.

Many women that make use of the health services, with complaints of migraines, gastritis, diffuse pains, and other problems, are living in situations of violence within their own homes.

The connection between violence against women and their health has become increasingly evident, although most women do not report that they are living in a situation of domestic violence. This is why it is extremely important that health professionals are trained to identify, attend to, and treat patients that come in with symptoms that may be related to abuse and aggression.

Violence and Mental Health

Women should not just be seen as the "victim" of violence that was provoked against her, but as an integral part of a relationship with the aggressor which takes place within a quite complex context, which at times becomes a kind of game in which the "victim" becomes the "accomplice."

Sometimes the woman makes a formal complaint against the aggressor at a specialized police station and then shortly afterward withdraws the complaint. Other times, she flees to a refuge, taking her children with her in fear of their lives, and some time later, returns home to live once again with the aggressor. These are situations that involve feelings, unconscious forces, fantasies, traumas, and desires of construction and destruction.

Trafficking and Sexual Exploitation of Women

In Brazil, most of the victims of human trafficking are women, supplying the international prostitution networks.

In 2002, a Study on the Trafficking of Women, Children and Adolescents for the purposes of Commercial Sexual Exploitation (Pestraf) identified that the Brazilian victims of international networks of trafficking in human beings were mostly adults. They are principally from the coastal cities (Rio de Janeiro, Vitoria, Salvador, Recife, and Fortaleza), but there are also cases from the states of Goias, São Paulo, Minas Gerais, and Para. The leading destinations are Europe (especially Italy, Spain, and Portugal) and Latin America (Paraguay, Surinam, Venezuela, and the Dominican Republic). Pestraf was coordinated by Professor Lucia Leal, of the University of Brasilia (UnB), and was the starting point for the work by the Mixed Parliamentary Commission of Inquiry (CPMI) by the National Congress carried out in 2003 and 2004.

Abuse and Sexual Exploitation of Children and Adolescents

The number of reports has increased significantly in recent years due to one of the main tools in combating sexual violence against children and adolescents: the spread of a phone line (0800-99-0500) for the National System for Combating Child and Youth Sexual Exploitation maintained by the Brazilian Multi-professional Association for the Protection of Childhood and Adolescence.

National Plan to Combat Child and Adolescent Sexual Violence

Set up with the aim of implementing a set of actions and targets to ensure the complete protection of the child and of the adolescent at risk of sexual violence, this plan sets out the mechanisms and directives to implement the policy of attendance established in the Statute of the Child and Adolescent. To accompany the implantation and implementation of the actions within the National Plan, the National Forum to Eradicate Sexual Violence toward Children and Adolescents brings together governmental and nonprofit organizations working in the prevention and combating of sexual violence against children and adolescents.

Violence against Lesbians

Homosexual women are even more vulnerable to the various forms of violence committed against women.

"Young people who discover they are lesbians and who are living with their parents are the ones who suffer most from violence. The family disapproves of the daughter's lesbianism and tries to impose heterosexuality as the normalization of the individual's sexual practice. In being without any power, the parents try to subject and to control the bodies of their lesbian daughters, using different forms of violence, such as physical and psychological mistreatment. And there is no shortage of accusations and threats, including being expelled from the house. The occurrences of violence are always in the sense of domination: it is the exercise of power, used as a tool for teaching, punishment, and control."

Violence against Elderly Women

Discrimination against women begins in childhood and continues through to old age. In some cases, it begins even before birth, in the selection of embryo's sex.

In the case of domestic violence against the elderly, the vast majority of victims are women. According to Maria Antonia Gigliotti, aged seventy-seven, president of the Municipal Council of the Elderly of the city of São Paulo, this "is to do with the mind-set of the patriarchal system, which considers that a woman is worth less than a man, however old she is. The financial factor is also important: elderly women are normally poorer than elderly men."

Sources

Violência doméstica, Portal da Mulher/realização do Instituto Patrícia Galváo—Comunicação e Mídia: http://www.patriciagalvao.org.br

Católicas pelo Direito de Decidir, Violência contra as mulheres, 2003: http://www.catolicasonline.org.br

Coletivo Feminista Sexualidade e Saúde: http:/www. mui heres.org.br/ violencia/documentos/saude_ mental_e_violencia.pdf

Violência contra a mulher e saúde no Brasil e em Violência, gênero y salud: http://mys.matriz.net/mys06/opinion/opi_06_01 p.html

Associação Brasileira Multiprofissional de Proteção à Infância e Adolescência (Abrapia): http://www.abrapia.org.br.

Cecria—Centro de Referência, Estudos e Ações sobre Crianças e Adolescentes: http://www.cecria.org.br

Ministry of Justicetraficosereshumanos@mj.gov.br

Marisa Fernandes, "Violência contra as lésbicas Maria, Maria, n° 0. Mais informações no site do =Um Outro Olhar": http://www.umoutroolhar.com.br

Site da Casa de Cultura da Mulher Negra: www.casadaculturadamul hernegra.org.br e do Instituto Socioambiental, www.institutosocio ambiental.org

About the Author

Celia Laratte was born in October 1956 in the city of Salvador in Bahia, Brazil. In 1976, at the age of twenty, she moved to the United States. She decided to leave her country because she was abused physically and psychologically at the time. She is now married and a mother of two, living in the city of New York and working at Rockland Psychiatric Center and Mental Health Association in Rockland County, helping people with mental disabilities for 28 years.